Andrew Unsworth

ACCESS 2007

In easy steps is an imprint of Computer Step
Southfield Road · Southam
Warwickshire CV47 0FB · United Kingdom
www.ineasysteps.com

Notice of Liability
Every effort has been made to ensure that this book contains accurate
and current information. However, Computer Step and the author
shall not be liable for any loss or damage suffered by readers as a
result of any information contained herein.

Trademarks
Microsoft® and Windows® are registered trademarks of Microsoft
Corporation. All other trademarks are acknowledged as belonging to
their respective companies.

Printed and bound in the United Kingdom

ISBN-13 978-1-84078-320-9
ISBN-10 1-84078-320-6

Contents

Using SQL 117

Creating Forms 125

Fine-Tuning Forms 141

Creating Reports   161

Sharing Access   179

Index   187

1 Getting Started

Starting up Access 2007 for the first time can be a daunting experience for the uninitiated. This chapter briefly explains how Access works and introduces Access 2007's new user interface.

Hot tip

Start thinking about your database now. What do you want it to do? What information do you need to keep?

What is Access 2007?

Access 2007 is the latest incarnation of Microsoft's popular Database Management System, or DBMS for short. By using Access 2007 you can:

- Store data using user-friendly forms

- Query the database for specific information

- Create attractively styled business reports

- Share data with colleagues over a network of computers

However, Access 2007 is much more than a means of entering and retrieving data. If you want to, you can build complete software applications limited only by your requirements and creativity.

And the good thing?

You don't need to be a computer scientist to use it. To be honest, you can use nearly all of Access's functionality without entering a single line of code. All that is required is a bit of patience, forward planning, and a clear idea of why you are building a database in the first place!

So What is a Database?

A database is simply an ordered collection of records. For example, the Rolodex on your office desk is a type of database. Open it up and you have the names, telephone numbers, and addresses of your business contacts.

In a computer, database information is organized in a much more structured way but the general idea is the same. Access keeps data in tables. A table is like the Rolodex – it contains all the data we need. Each row of the table contains data about a specific thing. In a Rolodex it would be a business card. The columns of the table help us to organize the data. Each column contains some specific item of data such as the address of a contact.

In the next chapter we take a deeper look at the way databases are structured and how to create them. For now, the rest of the chapter is devoted to getting you started with Access 2007.

The Getting Started Screen

Every time Access 2007 is launched you'll be greeted by the new, welcoming face of the Getting Started screen. Designed to do exactly as its name suggests, the Getting Started screen provides all the options you need to get the most out of Access 2007.

Below are some of the components that we will be discussing throughout this chapter.

Components of the Getting Started Screen

Office Button   Quick Access Toolbar   Help Button

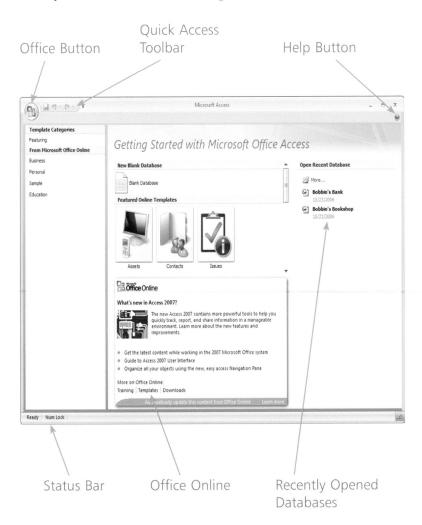

Status Bar   Office Online   Recently Opened Databases

The Getting Started screen changes dynamically as new content and features are introduced. For example, you will see new database templates added as Microsoft makes them available.

The Quick Access Toolbar

The Quick Access Toolbar provides quick and convenient access to commonly used commands such as Save, and is normally found at the top left of the Access 2007 screen.

By default the Quick Access Toolbar features only three buttons: Save, Print, and Undo. Although these are useful in themselves the choice of action is somewhat limited. As your confidence with Access 2007 increases you will soon want to have certain actions within easy reach. Luckily we can customize the Quick Access Toolbar and add or delete extra buttons.

Customizing the Quick Access Toolbar

1 Press the arrow to the right of the last button

2 Click a menu item to add that command to the Quick Access Toolbar

Adding an Action

Some of the most useful commands can be added to the Quick Access Toolbar using the menu to the right. However, many more functions can be added by clicking the "More Commands..." menu item. This launches the Customization dialog, which is discussed in more detail on the opposite page.

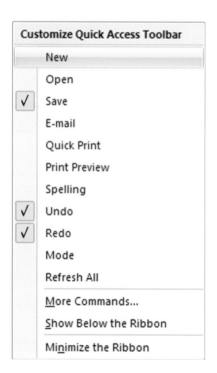

Customize Quick Access Toolbar
New
Open
✓ Save
E-mail
Quick Print
Print Preview
Spelling
✓ Undo
✓ Redo
Mode
Refresh All
More Commands...
Show Below the Ribbon
Minimize the Ribbon

Select the
actions to
add here

Click here to
see different
groups of
actions

Click here
to add the
selected action

Change the
order in which
actions are
displayed on
the Toolbar

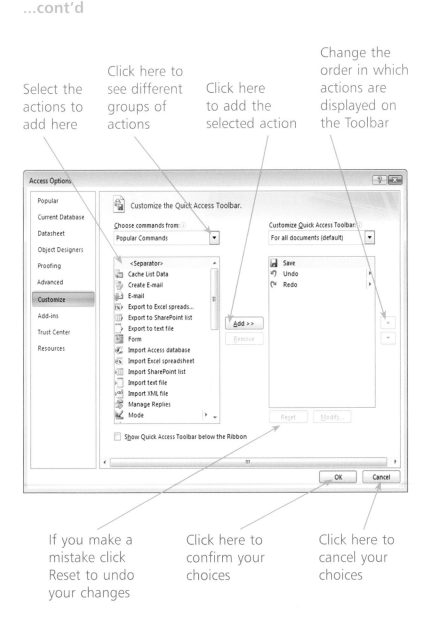

If you make a
mistake click
Reset to undo
your changes

Click here to
confirm your
choices

Click here to
cancel your
choices

Repositioning the Quick Access Toolbar

1   Click the arrow at the end of the Quick Access Toolbar

2   Click the "Show Below the Ribbon" menu item

Using the Office Button

The Office Button eases both file management and database administration tasks. Not only does it allow you to open and save databases; the Office Button can also be used to email databases to colleagues or perform maintenance operations on your database.

The Office Button is located to the left of the Quick Access Toolbar.

Opening a Database

1 Click the Office Button

2 Click Open from the Office Button menu

3 Find the database you want to open using the file dialog

4 Double-click the database name to open it

Click here to change directory

Double-click a file to open it

Type a file name here to search for it

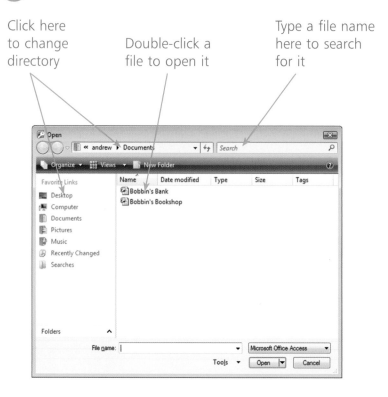

By default Access opens a database in a restricted mode of operation. Specifically, it disables the execution of Visual Basic for Applications code and macros. To enable all the features of the database click the "Options..." button located between the Ribbon and the main database window.

🛡 **Security Warning** Certain content in the database has been disabled   [Options...]

This displays a security dialog. Click the "Enable this content" radio button and then press "OK".

Saving a Database

① Click the Office Button

② Click the Save option

13

Beware

By default Access 2007 suggests the name 'Database' followed by a number: for example, 'Database1'. Avoid naming your databases in this manner, as having a lot of similarly titled databases hanging around your hard disk will cause confusion and will result in mistakes being made.

Creating a New Database

1 Click the Office Button to display the drop-down menu

2 Click the New menu item

3 Choose a name for your new database and enter it into the text field

4 Press the Create button

To save your database in a directory other than My Documents, click the Browse button.

Blank Database

Create a Microsoft Office Access database that does not contain any existing data or objects.

File **N**ame:

Database1

C:\Users\andrew\Documents\

Create   Cancel

Exiting Access 2007

Access 2007 is great, but despite its brilliance there will come a time when you want to switch it off. Here's how to do it:

1 Click the Office Button

2 Click the Exit Access button at the bottom right of the Office Button menu

Personalizing Access 2007

The Personalize options screen contains various settings that affect the way you view and interact with Access 2007. For example, you can decide whether or not you want Enhanced ScreenTips such as the one below to appear.

Table

Create a new blank table. You can define the fields directly in the new table, or open the table in Design view.

(?) **Press F1 for more help.**

1 Click on the Office Button

2 Click on the Access Options button located at the bottom right of the Office menu

Access Options

3 Click the menu items at the left-hand side of the Access Options dialog to switch between sets of options

4 Click on the drop-down menus to change option settings

Converting Older Databases

Access 2007 makes it easy to open and work with a database created with an older version of Access. The older database will look and feel exactly the same as a database created with Access 2007. The only drawback is that you won't be able to make use of the new features packed into Access 2007, such as the Multi-Valued Look-up Fields and the new Attachment data type.

Luckily, Access 2007 can quickly convert your old database to the new ACCDB file format so that you can use these features.

Beware

Once you've converted a database you will no longer be able to use it with Access 2003 or earlier versions of Access.

1 Open the database you want to convert

2 Click the Office Button

3 Click Convert

4 Choose a directory in which to save the converted database using the Save As dialog

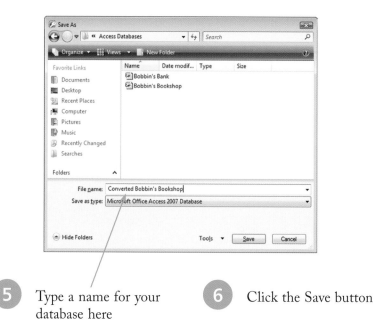

5 Type a name for your database here

6 Click the Save button

7 Click OK to get rid of the warning

Microsoft Office Access	
This Database has been upgraded to the Access 2007 File Format. The new database cannot be shared with users of Access 2003 or earlier versions.	
For more information about conversion, click Help.	
	OK Help

Converting Databases to Older File Formats

There may come a time when you need to share your database with others and as a consequence you may have to convert your Access 2007 database to a file format that will work with previous versions of Access. Perhaps your database is to be kept in a shared folder and updated by your colleagues directly.

1 Open the database you want to convert

2 Click the Office Button

3 Hold the cursor over the arrow at the right of the Save As command

4 Choose a file format to convert the database to

Access 2002 - 2003 Database
Save a copy that will be fully compatible with Access 2002-2003.

5 Use the Save As Dialog to navigate to the directory in which the converted database is to be saved

6 Type a name for the database in the "File name" field

7 Click the Save button on the Save As dialog

Beware

Consider your options carefully before you convert a database to an older file format, as you will no longer be able to use the new features of Access 2007.

17

Using Office Online

Office Online is an invaluable new feature of Access 2007 that quickly and conveniently helps you to search for new content such as database templates, improve your knowledge with online training programs, and keep your installation of Access 2007 up to date with program downloads and updates. In fact, Office Online is such a convenient feature that Microsoft have kindly incorporated it into the Getting Started screen.

Beware

The templates on this screen will be updated over time.

18

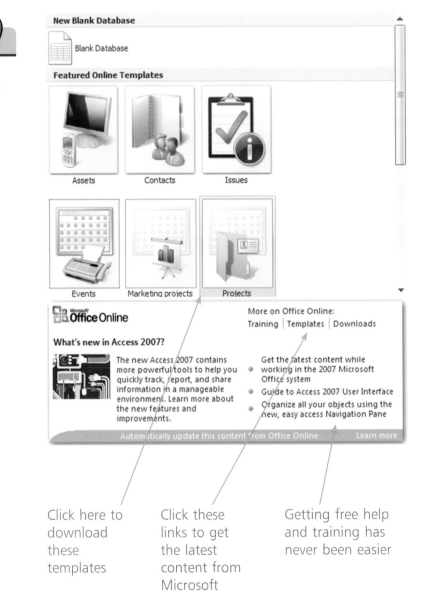

Click here to download these templates

Click these links to get the latest content from Microsoft

Getting free help and training has never been easier

Get Training Online

Although using this book will give you a good understanding of how to design and administrate databases effectively, Access 2007 contains many more features than could possibly be covered here. As you become more confident with Access 2007 you should actively search the Office Online training pages for courses that will help you to improve your databases and so keep one step ahead of the competition. To access the Office Online training pages simply repeat the following:

 Open the Getting Started screen by closing all the databases that are open

2 Click the Training hyperlink located under the label "More on Office Online"

More on Office Online:
Training | Templates | Downloads

3 Enter Access 2007 into the Search utility at the top of web page

Training

Search Training   Search 🔎 ▾

Search

4 Select a training course from the search results by clicking on its hyperlink

Searched Training for "access 2007"

 Want better search results? Tailor results to the Microsoft Office products you have installed.

Results 1-25 of 64, sorted by best match   Page: [1] 2 3 ◁ Next ▷

Up to speed with Access 2007
Help and How-to > Training > Access 2007

Up to speed with the 2007 Office system
Applies to: Access, Excel, Outlook, PowerPoint, Word

Hot tip

If you can't find the training you want, search again using related keywords. You might find that the help you need is covered in another topic.

19

Downloading New Content

New content is being made available all the time thanks to Microsoft's continual improvement of Access 2007. The content in question can either be conversion tools that let you work with databases created with older versions of Access, or product updates that add further functionality to your current installation of Access 2007.

 1 Open the Getting Started screen by closing all the databases that are open

2 Click the Downloads hyperlink located under the label "More on Office Online"

More on Office Online:

Training | Templates | Downloads

Get third-party downloads, services, and solutions
Explore Office Marketplace

Browse Downloads by Product

My Products | 2007 Office System | Office 2003 | Office XP | Office 2000

2007 Microsoft Office System

Desktop Applications
- Groove 2007   - 2007 Office system

Servers
- Live Communications
  Server 2005

Services
- Live Meeting 2005

Other Microsoft Office Programs
- Groove 2007

3 Access now opens a web browser. Scroll down to the section entitled "Browse Downloads by Product" and click the 2007 Office System tab once

4 Select the specific content you wish to download by clicking its link and then clicking the download button on the content summary screen that follows

Downloading New Templates

Access 2007 contains many professionally designed database templates and for many users these templates will more than meet their needs, albeit with a bit of tweaking. However, not all users have the same needs and if none of the pre-installed templates meets your requirements there is a good chance that a template on Office Online will.

 Open the Getting Started screen by closing all open databases

 Click the Templates hyperlink located under the label "More on Office Online"

More on Office Online:

Training | Templates | Downloads

 If a template catches your eye, click on its hyperlink for more information

Using Templates

Access 2007 ships with many high-quality templates that, for most people, can be used straight out of the box. For example, if your sole reason for investing in a Database Management System is to maintain the contact details of your customers then Access 2007's Contact template might be perfect for your needs.

The best way to see if Access 2007's templates are right for your organization is to open them up and see what they do.

Opening a Template

 Open the Getting Started screen by closing all the databases that are open

 Click once on a template category

Access displays the templates currently available within that category in the center of the Getting Started screen.

3 Select a template by clicking once on its icon

4 Click the Download button at the far right of the Getting Started screen

Assets

File Name:

Assets

C:\Users\andrew\Documents\

☐ Create and link your database to a Windows SharePoint Services site

[Download]   [Cancel]

Once a template is downloaded, Access 2007 prepares it for use and opens it automatically.

All Access Objects ▾ «

Tables ▲
- ▦ Assets
- ▦ Contacts

Queries ▲
- ▣ Assets Extended
- ▣ Contacts Extended

Forms ▲
- ▤ Asset Categories by Current V...
- ▤ Asset Details
- ▤ Asset List
- ▤ Assets by Location Chart
- ▤ Contact Assets Datasheet Su...
- ▤ Contact Details
- ▤ Contact List

Reports ▲
- ▣ All Assets
- ▣ Asset Details
- ▣ Assets By Category
- ▣ Assets By Location
- ▣ Assets By Owner
- ▣ Assets Retired
- ▣ Contact Address Book
- ▣ Contact Phone Book

Asset List

Asset List

New Asset   Collect Data via E-mail   E-mail List   Print List   Reports

ID ▾	Item ▾	Category ▾	Condition ▾
✱ (New)		(1) Category	(2) Good
Total	0		

Record: I◄ ◄ 1 of 1 ► ►I ►◦   No Filter   Search

Using the Ribbon

In previous versions of Access users created and interacted with databases by choosing commands from menus, but not any more. You interact with Access 2007 using a menu of icons called the Ribbon.

Rather than laboriously searching through an uninspiring collection of gray menu items, you can find the command you need more quickly and easily with the help of the icons of the Ribbon.

The Ribbon

Click the tabs to switch between different collections of icons

Click an icon once to use it

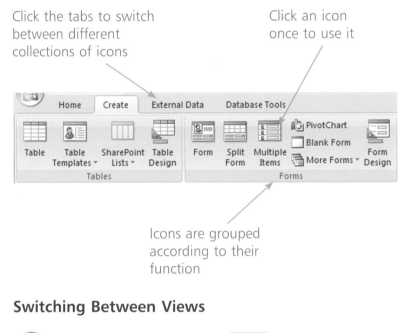

Icons are grouped according to their function

Switching Between Views

1. To switch between views click the down arrow beneath the word View

2. Select the desired view by clicking on its icon

Datasheet View

PivotTable View

PivotChart View

Design View

Using the Navigation Pane

Just as the old Access menu bar has been superseded by the Ribbon, so the Database Window has been replaced by the Navigation Pane. This can be found at the side of the main screen whenever a database is open.

The Navigation Pane makes finding Database Objects such as Tables and Queries easier by filtering them according to their type, the date they were created, and their group.

Filtering Database Objects

1 Click the down arrow at the top of the Navigation Pane

2 From the drop-down menu select a category to filter by clicking the category name once

3 Further refine your filter by clicking once on a group name

Navigation Pane with the "Query" Object type filter applied

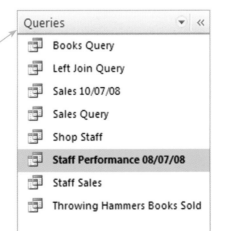

Using the Help System

Hot tip

Open the Help screen at any time by pressing the F1 key.

Screaming "Help!" is a common side-effect of working in close proximity to computers. Thanks to Access 2007's revised user interface it is now even easier to find the help you need.

As you've already seen, Office Online is a convenient means of finding help online, but that doesn't mean that you have to be connected to the Internet to get help.

1 Click the Help Button at the top right of the Access main window.

2 Click on a link to read an article

Searching for Specific Topics

1 Type a query into the Search text field and then click Search

2 Access will give more than one answer to your query. Choose one that interests you by clicking its link

2 Designing Databases

Correct design is key to the success and usability of a database. A little time spent on design now will prevent a lot of wasted time correcting errors later.

Relational Databases

It is perfectly natural for most people, when confronted with the daunting prospect of learning a new computer package, to scream loudly and run for the nearest exit in a blind panic. This is certainly true for a lot of newcomers to the world of relational databases, and yet it doesn't have to be so. Put simply, a relational database is a collection of tables containing data, which are related to each other through common fields so that use of the data is more efficient. The term "relational" refers to a way of modeling data that provides this efficiency. A lot of the confusion probably arises from the liberal use of jargon throughout the industry, much of it interchangeable.

Throughout this chapter we'll discuss the various concepts present in the relational model and look at how we can break the task of designing a database into smaller, more palatable chunks.

What is a Relation?

Despite its rather technical name a relation is nothing more than a table of data such as the one below.

Transactions				×
TransNumbe ▾	TransDate ▾	Amount ▾	TransLocation	▾
1	3/9/2007	£10.25	Billy's Bakery	
2	3/9/2007	£79.99	MB Sports	
3	3/10/2007	£45.99	Rockin' Records	
4	3/10/2007	£10.99	Schmoove Grooves	
5	3/10/2007	£23.97	Gromore Supermarket	
6	3/10/2007	£11.99	Billy's Bakery	
7	3/10/2007	£13.99	Schmoove Grooves	
8	3/11/2007	£99.99	Lassie Electricals	
*				

Record: I◄ ◄ 1 of 8 ► ►I ►✱ ✘ No Filter Search ◄ ▭ ►

To be used effectively an Access database will contain more than one table. Indeed, as we shall see later an Access database must contain at least two tables to be considered relational. Throughout this book we'll use the informal term "table" rather than relation.

In a relational database a table is based upon a particular concept or entity, typically something concrete such as a car, and holds data specific to that particular entity. For example, in a bank database we might have a Customer table that holds data about the customers of that bank, such as their names, their sex, and the amount of cash they have invested with the bank.

Another table we might see in a bank database is an Account table, which tells us the type of account a particular customer holds as well as the current balance.

A table consists of a number of columns, more formally known as fields, and a number of rows, more formally known as records. Logical links between tables are called relationships.

Fields

Field is the technical name for a column and is used to denote a specific type of data. For example, the Sex field below contains data denoting the gender of a customer. In a Car table we might have a Color field denoting the color of a car. Although it's tempting to refer to a field as a column this can cause confusion between fields and other objects. Throughout this book we shall refer to a field as a field.

Sex ▾
Male
Male
Female
Male
Female
Male

Records

A record is more informally known as a row and contains the actual data in a table. Whereas a field describes the type of data in a table, for example the sex of a customer, a record denotes whether a particular customer is male or female. If we think of a table as a description of an object, such as a car, then the rows of a table represent the actual cars.

Cars

Reg Number ▾	Model ▾	Engine Size ▾	Transmission ▾
Car1	Highlander	4.5	Auto
Car2	Highlander	3.0	Auto
Car3	Costa	1.6	Manual
Car4	Costa Sport	2.5	Manual
Car5	Siesta	1.0	Auto

Relationship Types

A relational database simply wouldn't be relational without relationships, would it? But what exactly are these relationships? And why are they so important?

A relationship is a logical connection between one table and another. The connection is made between a field in one table and a field in another table. For example, below we have two tables: a Branch table and an Account table.

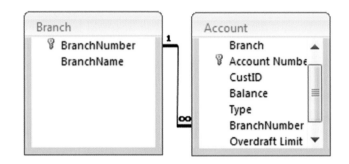

One branch of a bank will contain many customer Accounts. By relating the BranchNumber field of the Branch table to the BranchNumber field in the Accounts table we are creating a one-to-many relationship between the two tables.

There are three different types of relationship we can define between tables: one-to-one, one-to-many, and many-to-many. Each of them is briefly described below.

One-To-Many
We touched upon this relationship type in the preceding paragraph. We use this relationship type when one table, known as the parent (the Branch table in the above example), has more than one matching record in another table, known as the child table (the Account table, to continue the example).

One-To-One
This relationship occurs when there is a direct match between a record in one table and a record in another. For example, at the top of the next page are two tables: the Customer table and the Address table. The business logic behind the relationship states that a customer may only have one address at any one time. Therefore, every record in the Customer table directly matches a record in the Address table.

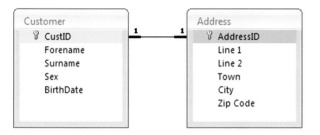

The two tables are said to have a one-to-one relationship.

Many-To-Many

In a many-to-many relationship records in one table can have many possible matches with records of another table, and vice versa. To model this relationship in Access we must create a third table, known as a Junction Table, and reduce the many-to-many relationship between two tables into two one-to-many relationships using the Junction Table as the intermediary. Below is an example of a Junction Table.

Below are the relationships for a typical database.

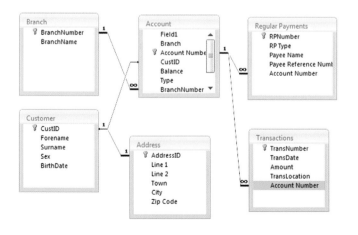

Database Design

Good database design is essential for creating a database that stores and retrieves information accurately and efficiently. Fortunately, the basic principles of database design are easy to learn and apply to your own databases.

In this chapter we'll cover just enough theory to get you going and keep you out of trouble, as a full discussion of database design would require an entire book in itself!

The Benefits of Good Database Design

There are many reasons why spending a little time on the careful planning and preparation of your new database is a good idea. Not only will it help focus your mind on the problem you're trying to solve, it will also reduce the number of errors in your database and thus save a lot of heartache later. Many painful, wasted hours have been spent trying to right a wrong database. A good database design can:

- Reduce the amount of redundant data

- Reduce the size of your database files

- Increase the efficiency of your Access database

- Maintain the accuracy of data stored within your database

Why Bother about Reducing Redundant Data?

Okay, so it doesn't sound that bad. But redundant data is actually something to be avoided at all costs. Redundant data is either data repeated in another table or data that could be calculated by Access so that it doesn't have to be stored at all.

For example, a table may have a field for a customer's date of birth and their age. In this case the age field is unnecessary as the age can be worked out by subtracting the customer's date of birth from today's date.

Having a slightly larger file size doesn't seem like such a bad thing, either. And when you only have a small amount of data in your database it isn't. However, as the amount of data stored in your database increases so will the length of time it takes Access to perform a query or report.

Before You Even Start Access

Riding the Development Life Cycle

Every project needs a plan, and the creation of an Access database is no exception. That's why, when they're not panicking about deadlines, database developers use the development life cycle as a guide. The development life cycle flows from top to bottom:

- Discover the requirements

- Design the database

- Create the database in Access

- Create forms and reports

- Test

In this chapter we're just going to look at the first three stages of the development life cycle, as it's these elements that will have the most bearing on the accuracy and effectiveness of your database. As you work through this book you'll develop your own ideas about the way your forms should work and what queries need to be performed.

Meet the Requirements

The first thing to do is to find out what the requirements are, which simply means asking the question: "What do you want the database to do?" It might sound an obvious question but many a computing project has failed because the designers didn't know what they should be creating!

Before you begin designing your database question the people who will ultimately use it to find out exactly what they expect of it. Find out what queries they need to perform and what reports they'll need to print.

What we're trying to find out are the user requirements, the *exact* needs of the end users. Note down their responses and keep an organized record of what the finished database should do. As you work through the different stages of the development life cycle refer back to these requirements to make sure you're still on the right track.

Designing Tables

Tables as Entities

What we're trying to do when designing a database is take a good, hard look at some aspect of real life and model it in a way that's compatible with Access. For example, a design for a bookshop database might model real-life entities such as customers and shop assistants, and the transactions that occur between them such as buying a book or making a refund.

A good way to visualize this is to imagine watching a film about the bit of real life you want to store data about – such as a bookshop – and then pausing it. Think about the actors in the scene and the data we might want to store about them.

A customer has a name and an address so we'd want to keep that information in our database for starters; we could use that to keep the customer informed of our special offers and latest stock. Similarly, we'd need to keep the same data on a shop assistant so that we could mail their pay check to them.

We'd also want to store information about the books on sale, such as the price, title, and author.

Books		
Title ▾	Author ▾	Price ▾
Throwing Hammers - A Retros	Ken Philips	$9.99
Stunning Creatures	Arthur Kent	$6.99
Crazy Mixed-Up Kids	Jimmy Scot	$6.99
King of Wishful Stinking	LM De'Pru	$6.99
Kane and Mabel	Jimmy Scot	$6.99
Cat On A Hot Tin Baking Tray	Arthur Kent	$6.99
Meadow Birds	Arthur Kent	$6.99
Rave on, Monty!	Jimmy Scot	$6.99
What Doesn't Kill You	LM De'Pru	$7.99
A Casa Called Home	Arthur Kent	$6.99

Imagine the scene you wish to model and jot down the names of the actors and objects that appear in it.

The name of your table will be the name of the entity you are modeling, "Customer" for example. Data about the entity, such as "Name" or "Sex", will be the fields of your table.

Primary and Foreign Keys

Choosing Primary and Foreign Keys

As we saw on Page 30, tables are related to each other by common fields. But how do we choose these fields?

Every table must have a field that uniquely identifies individual records. If we wanted to identify each record in a Car table uniquely, for example, we could use a field called Vehicle Identification Number, as a car's VIN is something that uniquely identifies it. Or if we wanted to identify each record in an Employee table we could use a field called Payroll Number, as an employee's Payroll number is something that uniquely identifies that person within a company.

A field that uniquely identifies individual records is called a primary key. Have a look at the fields you've chosen for your tables and see which field could become the primary key. There must only be one field that could possibly be a primary key within a table. If you have more than one field that could be a primary key you probably need to split the table into two or more tables. You'll see why later in the chapter.

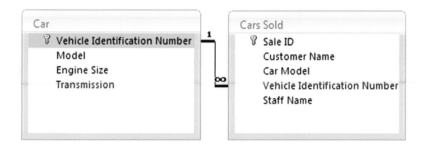

When we relate two tables we are making a link between a primary key and a foreign key. A foreign key is a field in a table that exactly matches the primary key of another table. For example, if we wanted to relate the Car table mentioned earlier with another table called Cars Sold that contained records of all the cars sold in a particular dealership, then we would include the Vehicle Identification Number in it as the foreign key. By relating the two Vehicle Identification Number fields, not only are we linking the information in both tables but we are doing so in a logical manner that makes sense.

Don't forget

No value in a primary key field can be null (that is, empty). Something has to be entered into it.

Beware

It is possible to have a primary key consisting of two or more fields that, when combined together, uniquely identify individual records in a table. However, this is not a good idea and should be avoided. The only exception to this rule is when you need to create a Junction Table to model a many-to-many relationship.

35

Don't forget

A foreign key in another table doesn't have to have the same name as the primary key to which it relates.

Fine-Tuning Your Design

Don't forget

If the database you are designing is not mission critical or does not contain vast numbers of tables it is not strictly necessary to normalize the tables past first normal form, though it is a good idea to do so.

Don't forget

If tables do not satisfy second and third normal forms then they must be split into two or more tables that do satisfy the normal forms.

Normalization

The final part of our table design is *normalization*. This is the process of gradually refining tables so as to protect the integrity and accuracy of the data stored within them. This also helps save disk space by reducing the likelihood of redundant data (data that is pointlessly repeated elsewhere). Normalization involves restructuring into the first, then the second, and then the third normal form.

First Normal Form (1NF)

In this form a field can only contain one value. For example, an address should be broken up into individual fields. You shouldn't put a whole address into one field.

Second Normal Form (2NF)

Every field in the table must be fully dependent on the primary key. For example, in an employee table with Payroll Number as primary key and two fields called Name and Department, the Name field is fully dependent on Payroll Number. This is because the two are intrinsically linked to each other, whereas the Department field isn't. An employee could work in any department but will only ever have one Payroll number.

Third Normal Form (3NF)

In third normal form non-primary key fields must not be dependent on other non-primary key fields.

Defining Business Rules

Deciding which tables we're going to include in our database and how they are related to each other is only one part of the design. In order to model more closely the real-life scenarios of our business we need to consider the business rules that govern them. Business rules, or business logic, are those often unwritten and unacknowledged codes of conduct that we follow at work every day. No one considers them except when designing databases because they are, pretty often, a matter of common sense.

For example, a business rule for a bank would be "Overdraft limits must be $0.00 or less", or "An account number must be n digits in length".

Write down the business rules that are relevant for your database, so that you can implement and enforce them as you progress.

3 Creating Tables

Tables are the foundations upon which your database is built. It is essential that you master the use and creation of tables in order to support both your database design and the database objects that will use them.

The Table Window

Even if you've used previous versions of Access the Table Window still needs some explanation. Thanks to a complete overhaul, switching between tables and finding the data you need is now easier than ever.

Components of the Table Window

Hot tip

Change how you view a table by right-clicking the tab of a table and choosing Design View or Datasheet View from the context menu.

Hot tip

Close all tables quickly by right-clicking the tab of any table and choosing Close All from the context menu.

Click the tabs to switch between

Select a field by clicking on its column heading

Closes the currently selected table

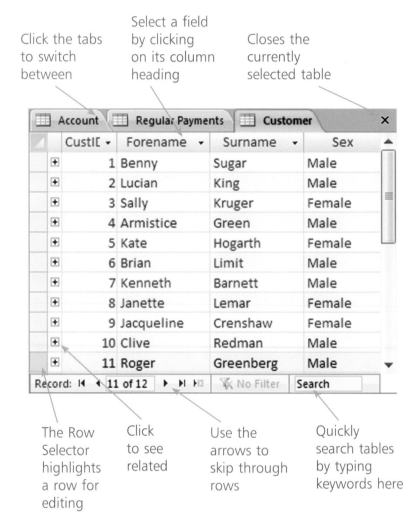

	CustIE ▾	Forename ▾	Surname ▾	Sex	
⊞	1	Benny	Sugar	Male	
⊞	2	Lucian	King	Male	
⊞	3	Sally	Kruger	Female	
⊞	4	Armistice	Green	Male	
⊞	5	Kate	Hogarth	Female	
⊞	6	Brian	Limit	Male	
⊞	7	Kenneth	Barnett	Male	
⊞	8	Janette	Lemar	Female	
⊞	9	Jacqueline	Crenshaw	Female	
⊞	10	Clive	Redman	Male	
⊞	11	Roger	Greenberg	Male	

Record: ⏮ ◀ 11 of 12 ▶ ⏭ ▶＊   No Filter   Search

The Row Selector highlights a row for editing

Click to see related

Use the arrows to skip through rows

Quickly search tables by typing keywords here

Hot tip

Save a table by clicking the Save icon on the Quick Access Toolbar.

Switching Between Views

Click the View icon to switch quickly between Datasheet View and Design View. You'll find it by clicking the Home tab on the Ribbon.

View ▾

Views

Using Table Templates

Although databases are designed for different purposes, much of the data kept in them is similar. For example, most businesses want to know the contact details of their customers. Table Templates exploit this commonality by providing ready-made tables that contain all the fields that most organizations will want to include in their databases. What's more, a table created using a template can be altered and fine-tuned to your exact specifications.

Don't forget

Once you've selected a Table Template you can change it at any time. Fine-tune it by adding or deleting columns, setting input masks, or specifying particular formats for data types.

1 Click the Table Templates icon

2 From the drop-down menu select the Table Template that best suits your needs by clicking on its icon

3 Click the Save icon in the Quick Access Toolbar

4 Type a name for your table and then click the OK button

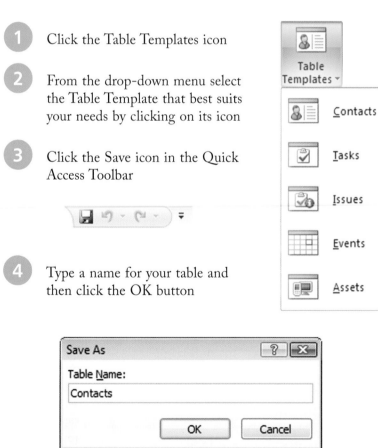

Using Datasheet View

Datasheet View is the default data entry view for Access 2007. Using the Datasheet View to build and manage your tables couldn't be simpler.

Creating a Table in Datasheet View

 Click the Create tab on the Ribbon

 Click the Table icon located in the Tables icon group

Press the Save icon on the Quick Access Toolbar

Enter the name of your new table into the Save Table As dialog and then click the OK button

Table1		✕
ID ▾	Add New Field	
* (New)		

Record: ◄ ◄ 1 of 1 ► ►ᴵ ►* | 🖫 No Filter | Search

Don't forget

Before you can save a table it must first contain at least one field.

Now you've created your table you'll need to add fields to it. Find out how to do that on the next page.

Note that Access automatically creates a field called ID. This can be renamed or deleted as your requirements dictate at a later time.

Adding and Deleting Fields

Adding Fields in Datasheet View

To make adding fields to a table that bit more interesting, Access 2007 provides two methods to do just that. The first can be done from within the table itself.

 Double-click the Add New Field column heading

BranchNumber ▾	Overdraft Limit ▾	Add New Field
131320	-£600.00	
131321	-£50.00	
131322	£0.00	
131321	£0.00	
131323	-£1,500.00	
131321	-£20,000.00	
131321	£0.00	

② Enter the name of your new field and then press Enter

We can also add new fields using the Ribbon.

① Click the Datasheet tab on the Ribbon

New Field	Add Existing Fields	Lookup Column	Insert · Delete · Rename
	Fields & Columns		

② Click the New Field icon

③ Access will now display a dazzling array of Field Templates to the right of the screen. Select a Field Template by double-clicking it

The trouble is, when you use the Ribbon method you have to rename a field manually. Learn how to do this on the next page.

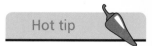

Hot tip

To move a field after it's been created, highlight it by clicking once on its heading. Then click and hold the left mouse button on the field heading again. A black stripe should appear along the left side of the field. Still holding the mouse button, move the black stripe to the required position. Then let go of the mouse button.

Hot tip

Don't waste time by repeatedly clicking the New Field icon. Double-click as many fields as you need from the Field Templates list in one go.

...cont'd

Renaming Fields in Datasheet View

There are times when it is necessary to rename a field that already exists. You might need to rename it because a field in another table already has that name.

Don't forget

You should always give your fields meaningful names so that you know what data they are supposed to represent.

For example, if a field holds data about a car's color then name it "Car Color" and not "Field 2".

1 Click the Datasheet tab on the Ribbon

2 Click the heading of the field you want to rename

3 Click the Rename icon

    ╨ Insert
    ╫ Delete
    ⊒ Rename

4 Type the new field name into the text box; then press enter to confirm you're happy with the changes

🖽 Customer				✕
CustID ▾	Forename ▾	Surname ▾	Gender	▲
⊞	1 Benjamin	Socorro	Male	
⊞	2 Lucian	King	Male	
⊞	3 Sally	Klein	Female	
⊞	4 Armistice	Golsdstein	Male	
⊞	5 Kate	Lewis	Female	
⊞	6 Brian	Revill	Male	▾

Record: I◀ ◀ ▶ ▶I ▶⊠ 🖫 No Filter Search ◀▶

Here, the Sex field has been renamed Gender

Deleting Fields in Datasheet View

    ╨ Insert
    ╫ Delete
    ⊒ Rename

1 Highlight the field to be deleted

2 Click the Delete icon

3 Access 2007 displays a warning. If you really want to delete the field, press the Yes button

Data Types in Datasheet View

Specifying a Data Type in Datasheet View

In datasheet view choosing a data type for your field is a matter of point-and-click simplicity. A full discussion of Access 2007 data types appears later in the chapter, but essentially a data type dictates the type of data that can be entered into a field. For example, if we assign the Number data type to a field then only digits can be entered into it. Typing a letter into it would generate an error message. Using a Number data type would therefore make it impossible to enter text into a field intended to hold telephone or bank account numbers.

Click here to change the data type

Check this box to ensure that every value in the field is different

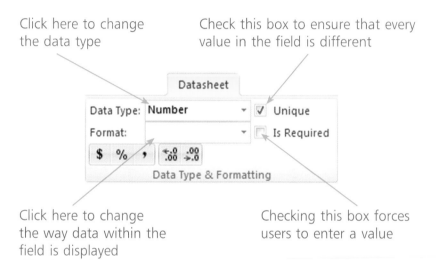

Click here to change the way data within the field is displayed

Checking this box forces users to enter a value

Formatting Number and Currency Data Types

The Data Type and Formatting icon group makes it quick and easy to apply specific formatting to Currency and Number formats. To apply a format simply click a value within that field to highlight it; then click the formatting icon relevant to your needs.

Applies Currency format

Inserts a comma after each thousand

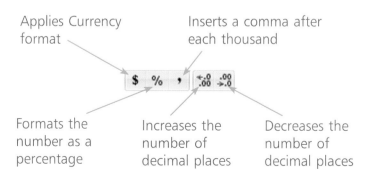

Formats the number as a percentage

Increases the number of decimal places

Decreases the number of decimal places

Using Design View

As easy as it is to create tables in Datasheet View, it isn't the most efficient way of building tables. Design View is far more time-efficient and gives a greater degree of control over the properties of your fields.

Design View gives you a clear view of the fields that make up your table and the properties and constraints you have placed on them.

Always try to use Design View when you first create your tables, only using Datasheet View to fine-tune your tables as you work with live data.

The Design View Screen

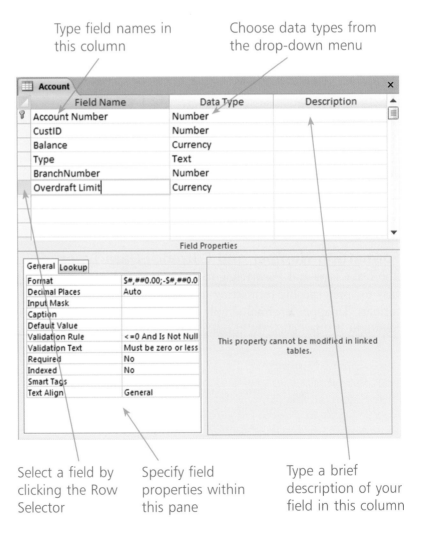

Type field names in this column

Choose data types from the drop-down menu

Select a field by clicking the Row Selector

Specify field properties within this pane

Type a brief description of your field in this column

Creating a Table

Design View contains everything you need to fine-tune and perfect a table.

 Click the Create tab on the ribbon

 Click the Table Design icon in the Tables icon group

3 A table opens in the centre of the Access screen in Design View

Table1			✕
Field Name	**Data Type**	**Description**	
	Field Properties		

4 Type a field name

5 Press the tab key to move to the Data Type column

6 Choose a data type from the drop-down menu

7 Press the tab key to move to the Description column

8 Type a brief description of the field

Data Type
Text
Memo
Number
Date/Time
Currency
AutoNumber
Yes/No
OLE Object
Hyperlink
Attachment
Lookup Wizard...

9 Repeat steps 4 to 8 until all the fields in your table have been entered

10 Click the Save icon on the Quick Access Toolbar

11 Enter the name of your new table into the Save Table As dialog and then click OK

Inserting a Design View Row

There are two methods of inserting a new row. Use whichever method you find the quickest.

Context Menu

1 Right-click the row underneath the point at which the new row should be inserted

2 Select the Insert Rows menu item from the context menu

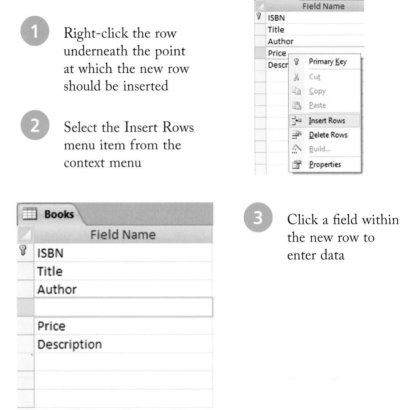

3 Click a field within the new row to enter data

The Ribbon

1 Click the Design tab located on the Ribbon

2 Click on the Insert Rows icon located within the Tools icon group

Deleting a Design View Field

There are two ways of deleting a row. Use whichever method you find the quickest.

Context Menu

1   Right-click the row that you want to delete

2   Select the Delete Rows menu item from the context menu that appears

3   Access will display a warning message. If you are certain that you want to delete a field, click "Yes"

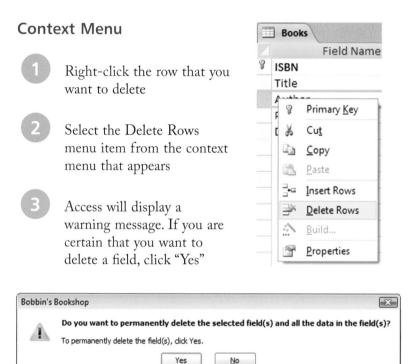

Bobbin's Bookshop

⚠   **Do you want to permanently delete the selected field(s) and all the data in the field(s)?**

To permanently delete the field(s), click Yes.

[Yes]   [No]

The Ribbon

1   Click the Design tab located on the Ribbon

2   Highlight the row you want to delete by clicking once on the row selector next to it

3   Click the Delete Rows icon located within the tools group on the Ribbon

⇥✕ Delete Rows

4   Access will display a warning message. If you are certain that you want to delete a field, click "Yes"

Setting the Primary Key

The Primary Key is a special field that is used to make relationships between tables. The value in a Primary Key field uniquely identifies the rest of the data in that field. For example, the Books table below uses the ISBN Number field as the primary key because it uniquely identifies a book. In Access, setting the Primary Key is simple.

Alternatively, you can also right-click a field name and select Primary Key from the context menu that appears.

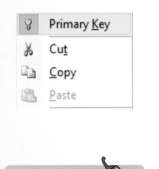

1 Switch to Design View

2 Highlight the field to be made a Primary Key

Books	
Field Name	**Data Type**
ISBN	Number
Title	Text
Author	Text
Price	Currency
Description	Memo

Hot tip

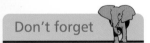

Delete a Primary Key by right-clicking the golden key icon and selecting Primary Key from the context menu.

3 Click the Primary Key icon

Don't forget

It's possible to use more than one field as the Primary Key. To add another primary key hold down the Ctrl key while following the steps detailed here.

When you click the Primary Key icon a golden key is displayed in the Row Selector for that field

Books	
Field Name	**Data Type**
ISBN	Number
Title	Text
Author	Text
Price	Currency
Description	Memo

Using Data Types

Using the correct data types will help others make sense of your database and prevent errors. The data type you choose for a field depends on the context and purpose of that field within your database. For example, if you want to record the date and time of a purchase then the Date/Time data type should be used.

Below are listed brief descriptions of the data types available within Access.

Text
The Text data type holds up to 255 characters of free text and, because it can contain numbers and letters, is very versatile. Examples of data that could be used with a text data type are names, social security numbers, or addresses.

Memo
The Memo data type is similar to the Text data type but can contain up to 65,535 characters. Rich Text Formatting can be applied to data in a Memo field to add a bit of color, change the alignment of text, and make lists.

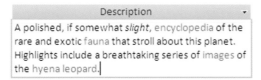

Number
As the name suggests, the number field is used to store numeric values such as ages or bank balances. The Number data type is very flexible. You can specify whether a field should use decimal places and, if so, how many. You could view values as percentages or display values in scientific notation.

Currency
The Currency data type is similar to the Number data type in that calculations can be performed on the data stored within it. However, the Currency data type can also display values in a format appropriate for a particular currency.

Hot tip

Users now have the option of using a calendar to input dates. To use it, click a cell in a Date/Time field and click the calendar icon that appears at the right-hand side.

Date/Time

Dates can be viewed in a variety of formats, regardless of how the user entered them. Access will automatically alter the date entered to suit the format that has been specified. Time can be viewed in 24- and 12-hour formats.

General Date	6/19/2007 5:34:23 PM
Long Date	Tuesday, June 19, 2007
Medium Date	19-Jun-07
Short Date	6/19/2007
Long Time	5:34:23 PM
Medium Time	5:34 PM
Short Time	17:34

AutoNumber

The AutoNumber data type is a special kind of number field whose value is incremented with every new record added to a table. It is designed to be used in fields where every value is unique and therefore its intended use is as a Primary Key.

Yes/No

Don't forget

The Yes/No data type is often referred to as the boolean data type. The two names are interchangeable.

The Yes/No data type presents the user with a checked box for Yes and an unchecked box for No. This field should be used wherever the user must choose between two possible values, such as true or false, on or off, up or down, etc.

Yes / No
☐
☑

OLE Object

The OLE data type allows users to store binary objects, such as Word documents or images, in a table. Unfortunately, the OLE data type is incredibly inefficient. Rather than storing a pointer to a file on disk it actually creates a bitmap image of a file that is often larger than the original file itself. It is far better to use the new Attachment data type.

Hyperlink

This data type is used to store the URL of a web page or an email address. Clicking on the URL launches a web browser that retrieves that web page or launches your email client.

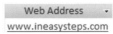

Web Address

www.ineasysteps.com

Using Attachments

This data type is used to store large binary objects such as images or other Microsoft Office documents. Better still, you can attach more than one file to a record.

1 Create a new field using the Attachment data type

2 Switch to Datasheet view

3 Double-click the paper clip icon

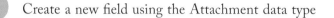

4 Click the Add button

Don't forget

The number in brackets next to the paper clip represents the number of attached files.

Attachments

Attachments (Double-click to open)

 Weekly Regional Sales.xlsx

Add...

Remove

Open

Save As...

Save All...

OK   Cancel

5 Use the File Dialog to navigate to the file you want to attach

6 Click the OK Button

To use an attachment, open the Attachments dialog using the above steps. Highlight the file you want to open and then click the Open button on the Attachments dialog. The dialog will open the file in its parent program. In the case of the above example, the "Weekly Regional Sales.xlsx" file would open in Excel.

Specifying Field Properties

As with most things in Access, every field has a set of properties that supports the design of the database by enforcing rules or controlling the way in which data is presented to the user on screen. The exact number and type of properties available depends on the data type of the field in question, but most field properties are the same for all data types.

Changing Field Properties

1 Switch a table to Design View

2 Click the text field of a field property

3 Some properties have an ellipsis "..." icon. Clicking this icon usually launches a wizard

Click here to change the way data is presented to the user

Text typed here will be displayed as a label on a form

General	Lookup	
Format	$#,##0.00;-$#,##0.00	▾
Decimal Places	Auto	
Input Mask		
Caption	Overdraft Limit	
Default Value	0	
Validation Rule	<=0 And Is Not Null	
Validation Text	Must be zero or less than zero!	
Required	Yes	
Indexed	No	
Smart Tags		
Text Align	General	

Over the next few pages we'll look at some of the more important field properties in detail and see how they can be used to ensure that only appropriate data is entered by users, or to present data to users in the correct format.

Using Validation Rules

Validation rules allow us to capture data in the exact ranges that we require. If you remember back to chapter two, we learned there that it's important to think of the business rules that govern a database. For example, a business rule for a bank's database might be "Overdraft limits must be $0.00 or less." It's common sense to have an overdraft limit that's less than zero, but unless we explicitly mention the fact to Access it won't know. In order that we have users entering the right values we have to validate the data that they enter.

 Switch to Design View

2 Highlight the field to be given a validation rule

3 Enter the validation rule here

General	Lookup
Format	S#,##0.00;-S#,##0.00
Decimal Places	Auto
Input Mask	
Caption	
Default Value	
Validation Rule	<=0 And Is Not Null
Validation Text	
Required	Yes
Indexed	No
Smart Tags	
Text Align	General

4 Move to the Validation Text field

5 Type a message

Default Value	
Validation Rule	<=0 And Is Not Null
Validation Text	Must be zero or less than zero!
Required	No
Indexed	No
Smart Tags	
Text Align	General

Hot tip

If there is already data in a table when you come to enter a Validation Rule, use the Test Validation Rules icon located in the Tools icon group to see if the existing data complies with the new rule.

Don't forget

The Validation Text is displayed in a dialog when users try to break the validation rule.

Creating an Input Mask

Input masks are primarily used as a means of validating data, as they force a user to enter data in exactly the format we require. For instance, if we want them to enter a date in mm/dd/yyyy format then that is what they must enter.

The Input Mask field is found on the Field Properties section of a table's Design View screen.

1 Highlight the field you want to give an input mask

Staff	
Field Name	**Data Type**
🔑 StaffID	Number
Forename	Text
Surname	Text
DateOfBirth	Date/Time
Salary	Currency

2 Type your input mask

General	Lookup	
Format	Short Date	
Input Mask	00/00/0000;0;_	[...]
Caption		
Default Value		

Click here to launch the Input Mask Wizard

Users must now enter data in the DateOfBirth field in the format demanded by the input mask, as shown below.

Gary	Hyman	5/5/1963
Richard	Farrimond	03/1█/___

Otherwise a dialog will politely point out the error of their ways.

Bobbin's Bookshop	✕
ⓘ The value you entered isn't appropriate for the input mask '00/00/0000;0;_' specified for this field.	
OK Help	

Setting a Default Value

Sometimes it is useful to have a default value for a field. There might, for example, be a certain value that needs to be entered more often than not, such as Male rather than Female.

For example, a marketing survey undertaken by Bobbin's Bookshop might show that women are more likely to buy a book from their stores than men. Therefore, it would make processing new customer details quicker if "Female" were the default value for the Sex field of the Bobbin's Bookshop Customer table.

1 Switch to Design View

2 Highlight the field to be given a default value

Customer	
Field Name	**Data Type**
CustID	Number
Forename	Text
Surname	Text
Sex	Text

3 Type your default value

General	Lookup	
Field Size	6
Format	
Input Mask	
Caption	
Default Value	"Female"
Validation Rule	

Open the table up in Datasheet View. The default value you entered will now appear every time you start a new record.

		6	Brian	Revill	Male
		7	Brenda		Female
*					Female

Using Indexes

An index is simply a reference that points to the actual physical location where a piece of data is stored. An index improves the speed with which Access finds and sorts data within a table.

The principle is similar to that of an index in a book. For example, you might want to find every place the word "index" is mentioned in this book. Rather than laboriously searching every page looking for "index" it makes far more sense to go straight to the back of the book and find the relevant pages in the index.

Don't forget

Any primary key fields will be automatically indexed by Access, but it is good practice to index foreign key fields too. In fact, it's best to index any field if it is unique or its values are likely to be different from each other.

56

1 Start off with the table that you want to create indexes for in Design View

2 Click the Design tab on the Ribbon

3 Click the Indexes icon

Property Sheet · Indexes

Show/Hide

4 Click the Index Name field in an empty row

5 Type the name of the index

Indexes: Sales			
Index Name	Field Name	Sort Order	
🔑 PrimaryKey	StaffID	Ascending	
CustID	CustID	Ascending	
ISBN		Ascending	

Index Properties

Primary	No	
Unique	No	The name for this index. Each index can use up
Ignore Nulls	No	to 10 fields.

6 Press the Tab key to move to the next field

7 Choose a field to index from the drop-down menu

Indexes: Sales			
Index Name	**Field Name**	**Sort Order**	
🔑 PrimaryKey	StaffID	Ascending	
CustID	CustID	Ascending	
ISBN		Ascending	

StaffID	
ISBN	
TransactionDa	
TransactionNu	
CustID	

Primary	No
Unique	No
Ignore Nulls	No

The name of the field to be indexed.

Hot tip

To delete an index, right-click the index you want to delete and then choose "Delete Rows" from the menu that

57

8 Choose the sort order

Indexes: Sales			
Index Name	**Field Name**	**Sort Order**	
🔑 PrimaryKey	StaffID	Ascending	
CustID	CustID	Ascending	
ISBN		Ascending	

Ascending
Descending

Index Properties

Primary	No
Unique	No
Ignore Nulls	No

Records can be sorted in ascending or descending order.

9 Identify the field as unique, if appropriate

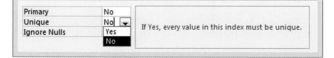

Primary	No	
Unique	No	
Ignore Nulls	Yes	
	No	

If Yes, every value in this index must be unique.

Creating a Lookup Column

With a lookup column users enter predetermined values into a cell using a drop-down menu, rather than typing in a value themselves. This helps minimize errors caused by incorrectly spelled words.

The values in a lookup column can either be drawn from another table (hence "lookup") or given to Access when the lookup column is created. The example below follows the latter option.

 Click a cell in the field you want to be a lookup column

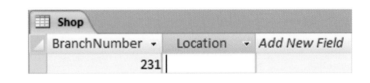

2 Click the Datasheet tab

3 Click the Lookup Column icon

Lookup
Column

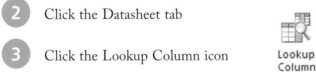

4 Choose this option **5** Click Next

6 Specify the number of columns you want to include in the lookup column

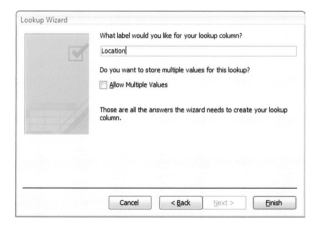

7 Type the values that users will be able to select from the lookup column

8 Click Next

9 Type a name for your Lookup Column

10 Click the Finish button

...cont'd

Click a cell in the lookup column and then choose a value from the drop-down menu to enter it.

Shop		
BranchNumber ▾	Location ▾	Add New Field
231	▾	
232	Jersey	
233	Richmond	
234	Washington	
235	Winchester	
*		

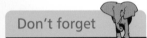

Don't forget

To more experienced database users, storing multiple values in one field might seem an utterly foolish thing to do. However, Access doesn't physically store the values in one field but instead hides them away in system tables as separate fields.

60

Using Multi-Valued Lookup Columns

A feature unique to Access 2007 is the ability to store multiple values in one field. This is handy if you have a range of options from which to select a value but more than one is appropriate. For example, suppose each branch of Bobbin's specializes in particular genres of books. Being able to enter each genre that's applicable to a branch into a multi-valued lookup field would be an ideal solution. To create a multi-valued lookup field follow the steps for creating a lookup column on the previous two pages, stopping after step 9. Check the box to allow multiple values and then click the Finish button as advised in step 10.

	Genre
✓	
	Do you want to store multiple values for this lookup?
	☑ Allow Multiple Values

Shop			
BranchNumber ▾	Location ▾	Genre ▾	A
231	Jersey	Comedy, Horror ▾	
232	Richmond	☑ Horror	
233	Washington	☐ Romance	
234	Winchester	☑ Comedy	
235	Redhill	☐ Fantasy	
*		☐ Erotica	
		☐ Crime Fiction	
		☐ Non-Fiction	
		OK Cancel	

Check the box of each value that you want to store in the field; then click OK. In the example to the left we see that the Jersey store specializes in Horror and Comedy genres.

4 Defining Relationships

Relationships between tables affect the way your entire database works, so it's important to get them right.

The Relationships Window

The Relationships window allows you to lay out your tables and specify relationships between them visually.

Tables are represented by blue rectangles

Primary Key fields denoted by golden keys

Click here to close window

Fields are listed within the tables

Relationships represented by connecting black lines

Opening the Relationships Window

1 Click the Database Tools tab on the ribbon

2 Click the Relationships icon

Adding Tables

If no tables have been assigned to the Relationships window, Access prompts you to add some with the Show Table dialog.

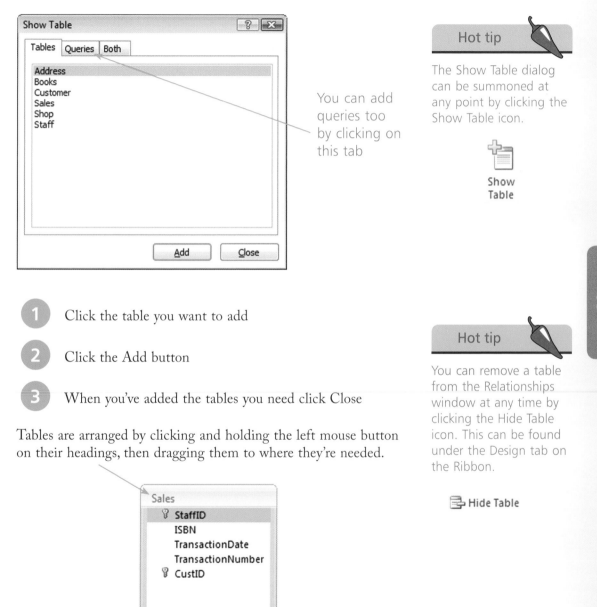

Hot tip

The Show Table dialog can be summoned at any point by clicking the Show Table icon.

Show Table

1 Click the table you want to add

2 Click the Add button

3 When you've added the tables you need click Close

Tables are arranged by clicking and holding the left mouse button on their headings, then dragging them to where they're needed.

Hot tip

You can remove a table from the Relationships window at any time by clicking the Hide Table icon. This can be found under the Design tab on the Ribbon.

Hide Table

The goal, once the relationships have been specified, is to have a screen that is uncluttered and can be easily read.

Specifying Relationships

Relationships are specified between tables by clicking and dragging a field (usually the primary key) to a corresponding field in another table. The two fields that you want to relate must share the same data type, or Access will display an error message.

1 Click and hold the field name of a primary key

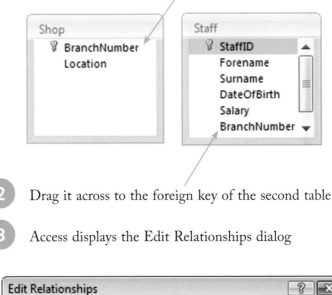

2 Drag it across to the foreign key of the second table

3 Access displays the Edit Relationships dialog

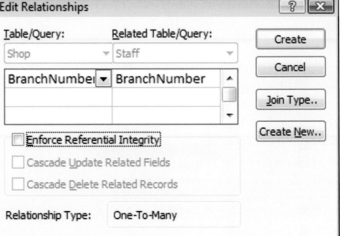

Hot tip

Notice that Access tells you the type of relationship you are specifying.

4 Check that the correct fields are being related

5   If need be, the fields can be changed by clicking here and selecting different fields from the drop-down menu

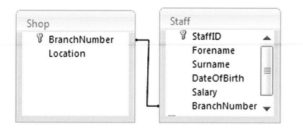

Edit Relationships

Table/Query: Related Table/Query:

Shop   Staff

BranchNumber   BranchNumber
BranchNumber
Location

☐ Enforce Referential Integrity

☐ Cascade Update Related Fields

☐ Cascade Delete Related Records

Relationship Type: One-To-Many

Create
Cancel
Join Type..
Create New..

6   Click the Create button to make the relationship

Shop
🔑 BranchNumber
   Location

Staff
🔑 StaffID
   Forename
   Surname
   DateOfBirth
   Salary
   BranchNumber

A relationship between tables is denoted in Access by a black line linking two fields, as shown in the screenshot above.

You may have noticed that the Edit Relationships dialog mentions the type of relationship created between the two tables. Even though Access works out the type of relationship automatically it's still important that you know the difference between the different relationship types in order for you to make the correct connections between tables.

Refer to chapter 2 to find out more about relationship types.

Hot tip

You can open the Edit Relationships dialog by right-clicking a relationship line and selecting Edit Relationships from the context menu.

Referential Integrity

When a record in a table is no longer needed it seems a matter of common sense to delete it. Also, in some situations it might seem like a good idea to change the value or data type of a primary key. However, this can cause update and deletion anomalies that interfere with the smooth running of the database and may result in errors.

To safeguard against this we can enforce referential integrity. This ensures that a record in one table only ever refers to an *existing* record in another table. To enforce referential integrity, first open the Edit Relationships dialog.

1 Select the relationship line by clicking it with the left mouse button

2 Click the Edit Relationships icon in the Tools icon group

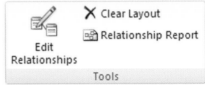

3 Check the "Enforce Referential Integrity" box

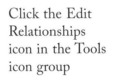

4 Check the two boxes directly underneath it

5 Click OK

The relationship line will now have a "one" symbol next to the parent table and an "infinity" symbol next to the child table, as can be seen in the image below.

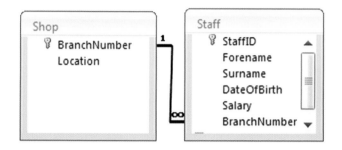

Cascade Update Related Fields
Checking this box forces Access to update all related child records when you change the value in a Primary Key field.

Cascade Delete Related Records
Checking this box forces Access to delete all related child records when you delete a record.

It's always a good idea to enforce referential integrity. Every table with a one-to-many relationship in the Bobbin's Bookshop database has referential integrity enforced.

More on Referential Integrity
Referential integrity is a type of *constraint* that is specified on a table to maintain the accuracy and consistency of the data in your database. But you might be wondering what enforcing referential integrity actually *does*.

By enforcing referential integrity you are asking Access to make sure that a record in one table that refers to a related record in another table only ever refers to an existing record.

Another type of constraint is the entity integrity constraint, which states that no primary key value can be null. When you make a field the primary key Access makes sure that a user inputs a value into it.

Specifying Join Properties

As well as specifying relationships between tables we can also specify join types. The join type is used by queries to decide which records should be displayed when the query is run. It can easily be selected from within the Edit Relationships dialog.

1 Click the line relating two tables

2 Click the Edit Relationships icon

3 Click the Join Type button

4 In the Join Properties dialog select the join type you want to use

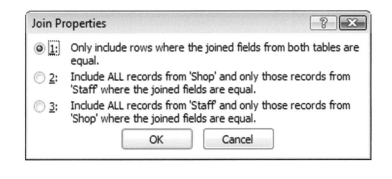

5 Click the OK button

More About Join Types

The Join Properties dialog lets you specify two different types of join – the Inner Join (option 1 of the dialog) and the Outer Join (options 2 and 3).

Selecting an Inner Join will ensure that only those records where there is an exact match between the related fields will be displayed.

In contrast, specifying an Outer Join will make a query display all the records from one table but only those records from another table where the related fields match. For example, running a query based on the tables below would display all records from the Customer table but only those from the Sales table where both CustID fields match. The results of such a query can be seen on the following page.

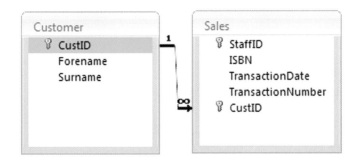

Left and Right Joins

When you specify an Outer Join between tables Access modifies the relationship line to include an arrow, the direction of which is dependent on the type of Outer Join you have selected.

An arrow pointing to the "many" side of a relationship, such as the one in the image to the right, indicates a Left Join.

A query based on a Left Join would display all the records on the "one" side of the relationship and only those records from the "many" side where there is an exact match. An example of a query based on a Left Join is shown below.

Left Join Example			
CustID	Forename	Surname	TransactionDate
1	Lee	Yates	
2	Ben	Atherton	8/7/2008
3	Kyle	Green	7/1/2008
3	Kyle	Green	7/10/2008
3	Kyle	Green	8/7/2008
3	Kyle	Green	8/7/2008
4	Malcolm	Billings	7/8/2008
4	Malcolm	Billings	8/7/2008
5	Luke	Bennett	8/7/2008
6	Jane	Lucas	
7	Geoffrey	Aaron	
7	Geoffrey	Aaron	
8	Michael	Lightfoot	7/10/2008
9	Moira	Harding	

Data in the CustID, Forename, and Surname fields are taken from the Customer table, as seen on page 69. The data in the TransactionDate field is taken from the related Sales table. Notice that not all the records contain data for the TransactionDate field.

Conversely, a query based on a Right Join would display the opposite. We would see a fully populated TransactionDate field but only some of the fields from the Customer table would contain data.

A Right Join is indicated by an arrow pointing to the "one" side of the relationship, as can be seen in the image below.

5 Working With Data

Entering Data

There are many different ways to populate your Access 2007 database with data. The most obvious way of inputting data is by direct entry – simply typing a value into a cell – but you can also copy and paste data from other programs, such as Microsoft Excel, or import existing data from another database.

Direct Entry

Hot tip

Move from field to field by pressing the Tab key.

Books	Customer	Sales	Shop	Staff
StaffID ▾	Forename ▾	Surname ▾	DateOfBirth ▾
1	Chris	Bones	11/8/1977
2	William	Boorman	5/3/1956
3	Victoria	Spinelli	1/7/1963
4	Harriet	Lascelles	6/12/1978
5	Gary	Hyman	5/5/1963
6	Richard	Farrimond	
✱			

1 Select the cell you want to give a value, by clicking it with the left mouse button

Books	Customer	Sales	Shop	Staff
StaffID ▾	Forename ▾	Surname ▾	DateOfBirth ▾
1	Chris	Bones	11/8/1977
2	William	Boorman	5/3/1956
3	Victoria	Spinelli	1/7/1963
4	Harriet	Lascelles	6/12/1978
5	Gary	Hyman	5/5/1963
6	Richard	Farrimond	
7	James		
✱			

2 Type in the value

3 Press the Tab key to confirm your entry

Repeat the steps above to enter data into another cell.

Inserting Rows

When you've finished entering data into the very last row Access will automatically insert a new row for you. However, you can manually insert a new row at any time.

 Click the Home tab on the Ribbon

	New	Σ Totals
Refresh All ▾	Save	ABC Spelling
	✕ Delete ▾	More ▾
	Records	

 Click the New icon in the Records icon group

Resizing Rows

 Place the cursor in between two rows

| Books | Customer | Sales | Shop | Staff |

StaffID ▾	Forename ▾	Surname ▾	DateOfBirth ▾
1	Chris	Bones	11/8/1977
2	William	Boorman	5/3/1956
3	Victoria	Spinelli	1/7/1963
4	Harriet	Lascelles	6/12/1978
5	Gary	Hyman	5/5/1963
6	Richard	Farrimond	
7	James		
*			

2 Click and hold the left mouse button. A black line will appear between the two rows

3 Move the mouse up to decrease the size of the rows or down to increase the size of the rows

Using the Clipboard

The Clipboard icon group, located under the Home tab, contains all the functions you need to copy and paste data.

The Microsoft Office Clipboard

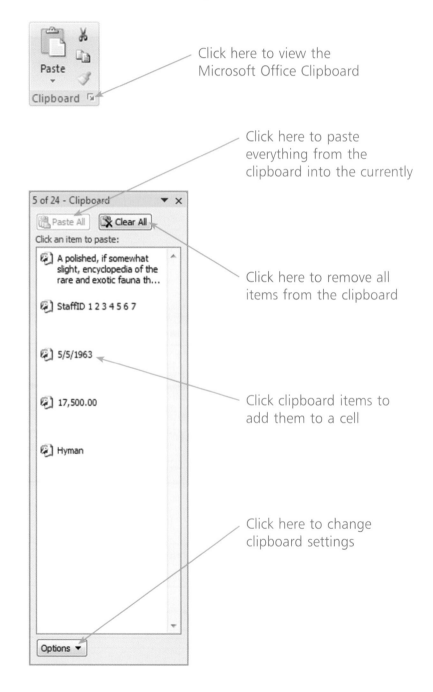

Click here to view the Microsoft Office Clipboard

Click here to paste everything from the clipboard into the currently

Click here to remove all items from the clipboard

Click clipboard items to add them to a cell

Click here to change clipboard settings

Copying and Pasting Data

The Clipboard Icon Group Explained

Clicking here pastes data onto the selected cell

Clicking here copies and then deletes data

Clicking here copies the formatting of the data, not the data itself

Clicking here copies data but does not delete it

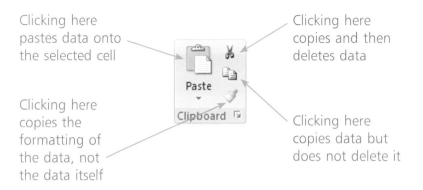

Copying Data from One Cell to Another

Forename ▾	Surname ▾	DateOfBirth ▾	Salary ▾
Chris	Bones	11/8/1977	$15,000.00
William	Boorman	5/3/1956	$20,000.00
Victoria	Spinelli	1/7/1963	$17,000.00
Harriet	Lascelles	6/12/1978	$13,000.00
Gary	Hyman	5/5/1963	$17,500.00
Richard	Farrimond	9/2/1972	

1 Highlight the data you wish to copy

2 Click the Copy icon in the Clipboard icon group

3 Click the cell in which you want to paste the data

4 Click the Paste icon to paste the copied data, as shown below

Paste

Harriet	Lascelles	6/12/1978	$13,000.00
Gary	Hyman	5/5/1963	$17,500.00
Richard	Farrimond	9/2/1972	$17,500.00

Copying Directly from Excel

It is now possible to copy data into your tables directly from Microsoft Excel in a few easy steps. Better still, you can copy multiple rows or columns of data from Excel into Access.

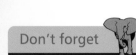

	A	B	C	D
12		11 Michelle	Khan	
13		12 Kyle	Green	
14		13 Ben	Atherton	
15		14 Lee	Yates	
16				

1 In Excel, select the cells you want to copy

2 In Excel, click the Copy icon (it's the same as the Copy icon in Access)

⊞		8 Michael	Lightfoot
⊞		9 Moira	Harding
⊞		10 Lesley	McCabe
⊞		11 Michelle	Khan
✳			

3 In Access, highlight the fields or rows that the data will be pasted onto by clicking field headings or by using the Row Selector

4 Click the Paste icon in the Clipboard icon group

Bobbin's Bookshop

⚠ **You are about to paste 3 record(s).**

Are you sure you want to paste these records?

[Yes] [No]

---

5 Click the "Yes" button on the dialog to paste the data

Copying Data to Excel

It is often convenient to use your Access data within Excel. For instance, you might use data from your Sales table in an Excel spreadsheet to see how well you've done that quarter. At one time using your Access data with Excel would have involved a time-consuming export task. With Access 2007 it can now be done in a couple of clicks.

 In Access, click on a field heading or, as shown below, a range of field headings to select the data you want to copy to Excel

Staff				
StaffID ▾	Forename ▾	Surname ▾	DateOfBirth ▾	Salary ▾
1	Chris	Bones	11/8/1977	$15,000.00
2	William	Boorman	5/3/1956	$20,000.00
3	Victoria	Spinelli	1/7/1963	$17,000.00

2 Click the Copy icon in the Clipboard icon group

3 Click the Excel cell in which the first field will be copied

	A	B	C	D
1				
2				

4 In Excel, click the Paste icon (it's the same as the paste icon in Access) to insert the copied rows into Excel

	A	B	C	D
1	Forename	Surname	DateOfBirth	Salary
2	Chris	Bones	11/8/1977	$15,000.00
3	William	Boorman	5/3/1956	$20,000.00
4	Victoria	Spinelli	1/7/1963	$17,000.00
5	Harriet	Lascelles	6/12/1978	$13,000.00
6	Gary	Hyman	5/5/1963	$17,500.00
7	Richard	Farrimond	9/2/1972	$17,500.00

Beware

Data copied into Excel may be formatted according to the default formatting currently selected in Excel. This means that your data from Access might look different when viewed in Excel. Consult your Microsoft Excel documentation if you want to change the default formatting.

Importing Data from Excel

There are many reasons why you might want to import data from an Excel file. Perhaps part of your database is used to keep tabs on the productivity of your sales people, who record their sales in an Excel spreadsheet. Rather than type their results into Access using a printed Excel spreadsheet you could simply append them to a table. Or maybe you've outgrown Excel and need to move a number of worksheets to Access. You could use the data in individual worksheets to create completely new tables in Access.

When importing from Excel it's important that the spreadsheet you are importing data from is in the correct format. Set up the spreadsheet so that each row in Excel is equivalent to a row in Access and each column is equivalent to a field, as shown below.

	A	B	C
1	CustID	Forename	Surname
2	1	Benjamin	Socorro
3	2	Lucian	King
4	3	Sally	Klein
5	4	Armistice	Golsdstein
6	5	Kate	Lewis
7	6	Brian	Revill

Importing Data into a New Table

 1 Click the External Data tab on the Ribbon

| Home | Create | External Data | Database Tools |

 2 Click the Excel icon in the Import icon group

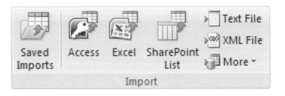

Saved Imports | Access | Excel | SharePoint List | Text File | XML File | More ▾

Import

Get External Data - Excel Spreadsheet

Select the source and destination of the data

Specify the source of the data.

File name: C:\Users\   [Browse...]

Specify how and where you want to store the data in the current database.

○ **Import the source data into a new table in the current database.**
If the specified table does not exist, Access will create it. If the specified table already exists, Access might overwrite its contents with the imported data. Changes made to the source data will not be reflected in the database.

○ **Append a copy of the records to the table:** [Address ▾]
If the specified table exists, Access will add the records to the table. If the table does not exist, Access will create it. Changes made to the source data will not be reflected in the database.

3 Make sure the "Import the source data into a new table..." radio button is selected

4 Click the Browse button to display the file dialog

File Open

◄ ○ ▾ | « Excel Files | ▾ | ↔ | Search 🔍

Organize ▾   Views ▾   New Folder   ⑦

Favorite Links

Name	Date modified	Type	Size	Tags
1st Quarter Sales				
2nd Quarter Sales				
3rd Quarter Sales				
Customer Spreadsheet				
Market Segmentation				
New Customers				
Weekly Regional Sales				

- Desktop
- Computer
- Documents
- Pictures
- Music
- Recently Changed
- Searches

Folders ∧

File name: New Customers   ▾   Microsoft Excel ▾

Tools ▾   [Open ▾]   [Cancel]

5 Use the file dialog to find the Excel file you want to import data from

6 Click Open

7 Click OK

...cont'd

8 Select the worksheet to be imported by clicking on it

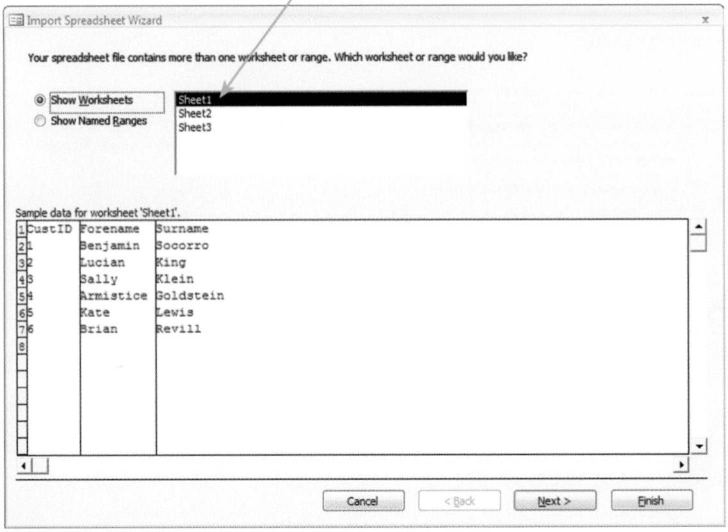

9 Click the Next button

10 Check the box if you want the values in the first row to be used as field names in your new table

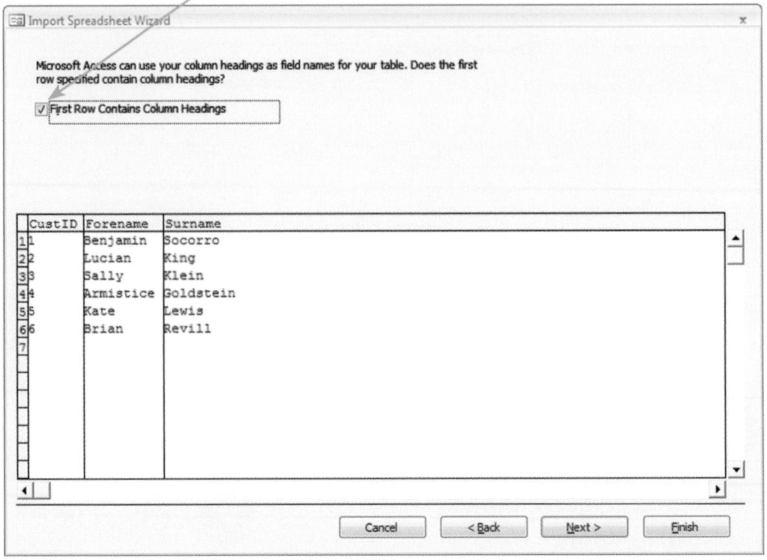

11. Click the Next button
12. Click here to change field names
13. Click here to change data types

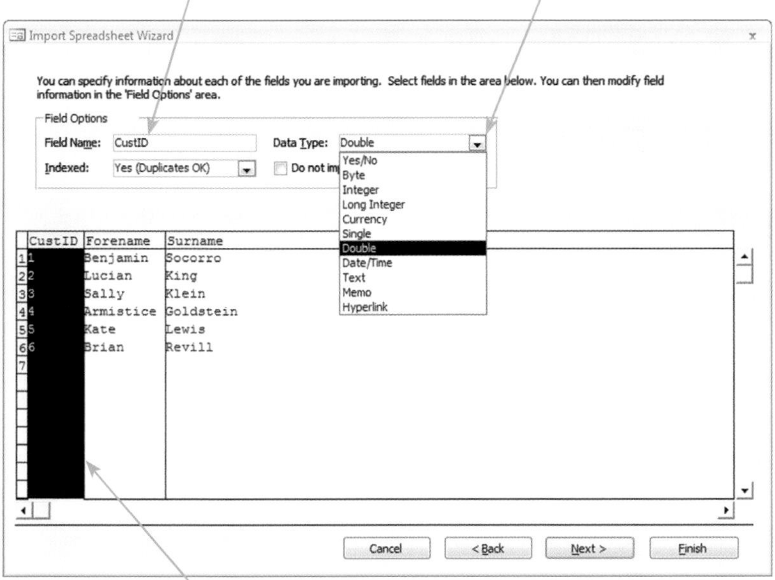

14. Click a column to select that field
15. Click the Next button
16. Use the drop-down menu to choose a primary key or let Access create one for you

Beware

Think carefully about the selections you make on this page. It's quicker and easier to choose the right data types now than later.

Hot tip

When you click a column to select it the background for that column will turn black.

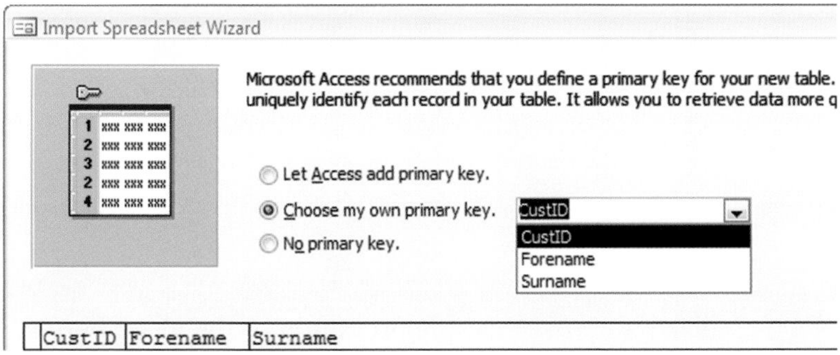

...cont'd

 Type a name for your new table

Import Spreadsheet Wizard

That's all the information the wizard needs to import your data.

Import to Table:

New Customers

 Click the Next button

19 Check this box if you want to import from the same worksheet in the future

Get External Data - Excel Spreadsheet

Save Import Steps

Finished importing file 'C:\Excel Files\New Customers.xlsx' to table 'New Customers'.

Do you want to save these import steps? This will allow you to quickly repeat the operation without using the wizard.

☑ Save import steps

Save as: Import-New Customers

Description: Imports data from the New Customers Spreadsheet

Create an Outlook Task.

If you regularly repeat this saved operation, you can create an Outlook task that reminds you when it is time to repeat this operation. The Outlook task will include a Run Import button that runs the import operation in Access.

☑ Create Outlook Task

Hint: To create a recurring task, open the task in Outlook and click the Recurrence button on the Task tab.

Manage Data Tasks... | Save Import | Cancel

20 Click either the Save Import button or the Close button

Importing Data from Access

There are two ways of working with other Access databases. The first is to import database objects, such as tables, queries, and forms, from a database. The second is to link to a table in another Access database.

The first method gives us a tremendous degree of control over what we import. For example, we can import either a table and its data, or just the structure of the table and no data.

Importing Database Objects

1 Click the External Data tab on the Ribbon

2 Click the Access icon in the Import icon group

3 Make sure the "Import tables, queries…" option is selected

4 Click the Browse button

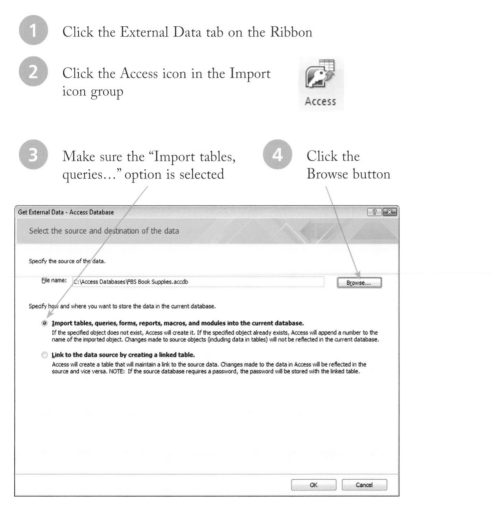

5 Use the file dialog to select the database to import

6 Click the OK button

...cont'd

Hot tip

You can select more than
one table in the Import
Objects dialog.

7 Click the tabs to see
different database objects

8 Click the names of the
objects to import

Import Objects

Tables | Queries | Forms | Reports | Macros | Modules

FBS Sales Contacts
Marketing Info
Sales Charts
Stock List

OK

Cancel

Select All

Deselect All

Options >>

Import
- ☑ Relationships
- ☐ Menus and Toolbars
- ☐ Import/Export Specs
- ☐ Nav Pane Groups

Import Tables
- ◉ Definition and Data
- ○ Definition Only

Import Queries
- ◉ As Queries
- ○ As Tables

9 Click the
Options button

10 Set import options

11 Click OK

12 Check the "Save import steps" box if you plan on repeating
the same import in the future

Do you want to save these import steps? This will allow you to quickly repeat

☑ Save import steps

Save as: Import-FBS Book Supplies

13 Click the Close button

Linking to Access Databases

Linking to Another Access Database

Repeatedly importing data from one database into another is inefficient and wasteful. If there is data in another database that you need to use regularly it might be best to link it with a table in your own database. By linking two tables a connection is made between the original table (the source) and a table in your own database (the destination). However, it is only possible to link tables and not forms, queries, reports, etc.

Don't forget

Once a table is linked to a counterpart in another database you can view and change the values in it as you like. The changes you make will be seen in both tables. The only thing you can't do is change the structure of the table.

1 Click the External Data tab on the Ribbon

2 Click the Access icon in the Import icon group

3 Click the Browse button on the Get External Data dialog and use the File Dialog to select the database you want to link to

---

Get External Data - Access Database

Select the source and destination of the data

Specify the source of the data.

File name: C:\Access Databases\FBS Book Supplies.accdb   Browse...

Specify how and where you want to store the data in the current database.

○ **Import tables, queries, forms, reports, macros, and modules into the current database.**
  If the specified object does not exist, Access will create it. If the specified object already exists, Access will append a number to the name of the imported object. Changes made to source objects (including data in tables) will not be reflected in the current database.

◉ **Link to the data source by creating a linked table.**
  Access will create a table that will maintain a link to the source data. Changes made to the data in Access will be reflected in the source and vice versa. NOTE: If the source database requires a password, the password will be stored with the linked table.

OK   Cancel

---

4 Click here to ensure you're linking to a database and not importing from it

5 Click OK

...cont'd

Hot tip

You can select more than one table in the Link Tables dialog.

6 Use the Link Tables dialog to select the tables you want to link to in the source database. Click on the name of a table to select it

Link Tables		
Tables		
FBS Sales Contacts		OK
Marketing Info		Cancel
Sales Charts		Select All
Stock List		Deselect All

Don't forget

You can update linked tables at any time by using the Linked Table Manager. The process is described on page 185.

7 Click OK

The names of the linked tables now appear in the Navigation Pane and they can be opened and used just like any other table.

Linked tables are distinguished from other tables by an arrow to the left of the table name, as in the image to the right.

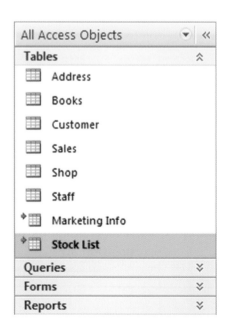

All Access Objects

Tables
- Address
- Books
- Customer
- Sales
- Shop
- Staff
- Marketing Info
- **Stock List**

Queries

Forms

Reports

Managing Import Tasks

If you chose to save your import steps, you may have wondered where they ended up. You can find them via the Manage Data Tasks dialog. You can view this dialog by clicking the Saved Imports icon in the Import icon group.

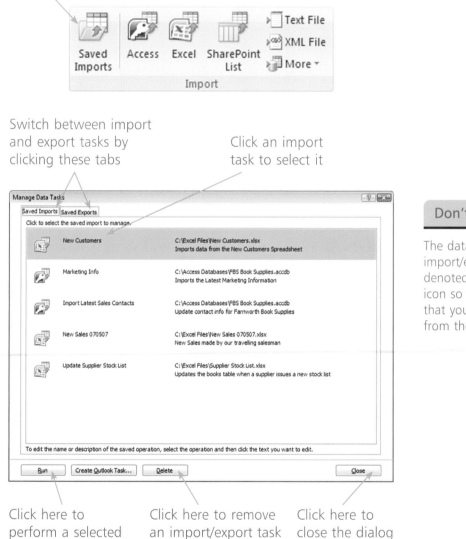

Switch between import and export tasks by clicking these tabs

Click an import task to select it

Click here to perform a selected import/export task

Click here to remove an import/export task permanently

Click here to close the dialog

Click the Create Outlook Task button if you'd like to be reminded to repeat an import/export task. This is useful if there is a particular import/export task that you need to perform often.

Collecting Data with Email

A fantastic new feature of Access 2007 is the ability to collect data using email. Access creates an HTML or Infopath form based on information that you provide and emails it to recipients that you select. When the recipients of the email reply you can either manage the replies yourself or have Access do it for you. This feature can be handy if you want to update your contacts or customer information regularly, or want to conduct a customer satisfaction survey.

To use this feature you must have Outlook 2007 installed.

1 Click the External Data tab on the Ribbon

2 Click the Create E-mail icon in the Collect Data icon group

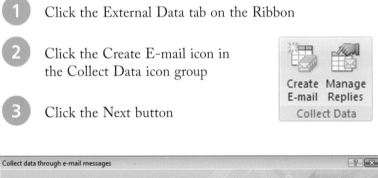

3 Click the Next button

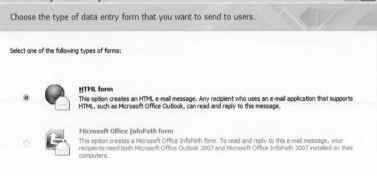

4 Click to choose between a HTML form or an Infopath form

If you're unsure which form type to select, choose an HTML form. If you use an Infopath form then the recipients of your email must have both Outlook 2007 and Infopath 2007 on their computers. This is unlikely to be the case for the vast majority of your recipients, and for that reason it is best not to use Infopath forms. The only requirement for using an HTML form is that your recipients must have an email client that can open HTML emails, which in this day and age is quite likely.

5 Click the Next button

6 Decide whether you want to add new data to a table or update existing data

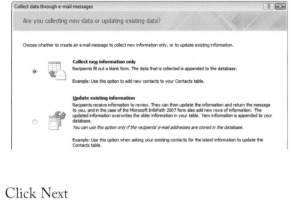

Don't forget

The primary key for a table will automatically be assigned to the email. The primary key must be included in the email and cannot be removed.

7 Click Next

8 Highlight a field and then click the right arrow to add it to the email form

9 Use the up and down arrows to change the order in which the fields are displayed

...cont'd

10 Click the Next button

11 To have data automatically added to your tables when people reply, check this box

Hot tip

By default your replies will be placed in an Outlook folder titled "Access Data Collection Replies". If you'd rather they went elsewhere you can specify a different location by clicking the blue link and selecting a folder from the dialog that appears.

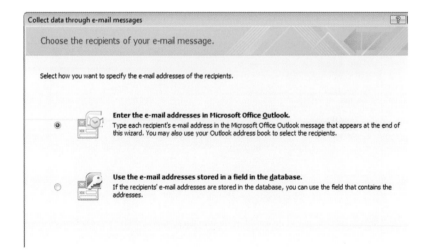

12 Click the Next button

13 Choose between entering the email addresses yourself or using a field from the table in your database

14 Click the Next button

Alter the Subject line and the body text as you wish

 Click the Next button

Click the Create button

...cont'd

 Check your email, enter the names of your recipients, and then click the Send icon

Importing Data From Outlook 2007

Access can automatically add data collected by email to a table, but if you prefer you can add data manually.

1 Open the Access Data Collection Replies email folder within Outlook 2007

 Right-click the email you want to import

3 From the menu choose Export Data To Microsoft Access

4 Review the data to be imported in the Export Data To Microsoft Access dialog and then click OK

Managing Replies

The Manage Replies dialog is useful if you've changed your mind about manually processing replies and want to have Access process them automatically instead. Or it could be that you want to resend or delete an email message.

Click here for email processing options

Click here to delete the message permanently

Click here to resend the message

Click here to exit the dialog

Clicking the Message Options button opens the Collecting Data Using Email Options dialog. This dialog lets you specify the number of replies to be processed and also lets you specify a deadline for the replies. This is useful if you've sent out a questionnaire and need to analyze the data on a specific date.

Don't forget

To open the Manage Replies dialog you need to click the Manage Replies icon. This can be found under the External Data tab in the Collect Data icon group.

Filtering Data

As you'll see in Chapter 6, queries are a powerful means of selecting records according to strict criteria. But sometimes we just want to limit the amount of data on screen. For example, in a sales table we might only want to view data about a particular product. Filters are a fast way of doing this and can be found under the Home tab on the Ribbon.

The Sort & Filter Icon Group Explained

Don't forget

Advanced filters work in a similar way to queries and for that reason won't be dealt with in this book. Once you've worked through Chapter 6 and are confident with the use of queries, applying advanced filters will be a doddle.

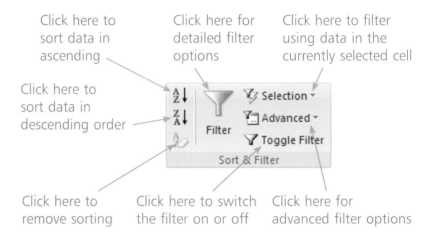

Click here to sort data in ascending

Click here for detailed filter options

Click here to filter using data in the currently selected cell

Click here to sort data in descending order

Click here to remove sorting

Click here to switch the filter on or off

Click here for advanced filter options

Filtering by Selection

The simplest method of filtering data is to filter by selection. This restricts the number of records seen on screen according to simple criteria. For example, we could apply a filter to the Books table so that Access only displays the records where Jimmy Scot is the author, as shown in the example below.

1 Click the cell containing the data you want for the filter

Books		
Title	Author	Price
Throwing Hammers - A Retros|	Ken Philips	$9.99
Stunning Creatures	Arthur Kent	$6.99
Crazy Mixed-Up Kids	Jimmy Scot|	$6.99
King of Wishful Stinking	LM De'Pru	$7.99
Kane and Mabel	Jimmy Scot	$6.99
Craze the Corinthian	LM De'Pru	$7.99
Meadow Birds	Arthur Kent	$6.99

2 Click the Selection icon in the Sort & Filter icon group

3 Click a filtering option from the filter menu that appears

> **✓ Selection ▾**
>
> Equals "Jimmy Scot"
>
> Does **N**ot Equal "Jimmy Scot"
>
> Con**t**ains "Jimmy Scot"
>
> **D**oes Not Contain "Jimmy Scot"

As can be seen below, when the filter is applied the only records in the Books table are those where Jimmy Scot is the author.

Title	Author	Price
Kane and Mabel	Jimmy Scot	$6.99
Rave on, Monty!	Jimmy Scot	$6.99
Crazy Mixed-Up Kids	Jimmy Scot	$6.99

Books

Applying a Detailed Filter

Filtering by selection might be fast but it is limited. What if we wanted to restrict the records on screen using two data values rather than one? We might, for example, want to see records where either Jimmy Scot or Arthur Kent is the author. In this case we would use a detailed filter.

1 Click a cell in the field that contains the data you want to filter

2 Click the Filter icon

3 Check the boxes for the values you want the filter to select

4 Click OK

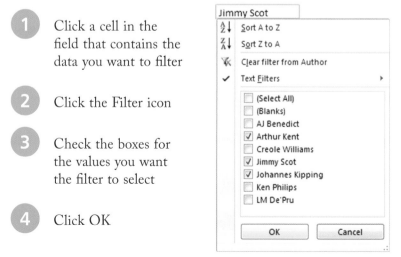

Totalling Columns

Access 2007 allows you to total the values in a column. You can use the Totals function to sum the values in a column or find averages. It can even subject the data to statistical functions more commonly associated with Excel, for example finding the standard deviation or variance of the values in a column.

In the example below we can see the Sum function being applied to a query that lists the books sold by Bobbin's Bookshop on a specific date. Applying the Sum function will tell us how much money the bookshop made on that day.

 **Don't forget**

The Records icon group can be found under the Home tab on the Ribbon.

1 Click the Totals icon in the Records icon group

Σ Totals

2 Select a field by clicking a cell in the "Total" row that appears at the foot of the table

Title	Author	Price
Kane and Mabel	Jimmy Scot	$6.99
Meadow Birds	Arthur Kent	$6.99
Rave on, Monty!	Jimmy Scot	$6.99
What Doesn't Kill You	AJ Benedict	$6.99
Nursing Red Mercury	AJ Benedict	$6.99
Memoirs of a Superstar	Creole Williams	$6.99
Stunning Creatures	Arthur Kent	$6.99
Crazy Mixed-Up Kids	Jimmy Scot	$6.99
Total		

3 Click the down arrow

4 Select the function you want to use from the drop-down menu

None
Sum
Average
Count
Maximum
Minimum
Standard Deviation
Variance

The result of applying the function appears in the cell.

Crazy Mixed-Up Kids	Jimmy Scot	$6.99
Total		$55.92

Spell-Checking Data

Not only is it possible to check the spelling in a field, you can also choose a specific dictionary to check it against.

Spell-checking data can be a good and a bad thing. It is of most use when checking descriptive data, such as that in a memo field, rather than an arbitrary text field that could contain a surname (for example). As everyone who has ever used Word will know, spell-checkers take great exception to names that they aren't familiar with and will offer a range of entirely unsuitable alternatives. Unfortunately, unless you specifically highlight a cell, the spell-checker hunts for mistakes field by field, starting with the first record and working its way down to the last, so be sure to check the data value under scrutiny before taking its advice.

1   Click the Spelling
    icon

2   Use the Spelling
    dialog to locate
    misspelled words

Misspelled words
appear here

Suggested alternatives to the
misspelled word appear here

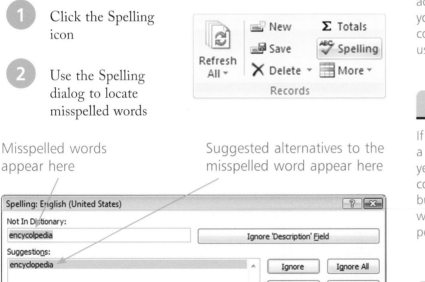

3   To change the current spelling, highlight one of the
    suggested spellings by clicking it

4   Click the Change button

Don't forget

The "Records" icon group can be found by clicking the Home tab on the Ribbon.

Beware

To ensure that you have accurate spellings for your region check the correct dictionary is in use by the spell-checker.

Hot tip

If the spell-checker claims a word is misspelled yet you know it to be correct, click the Add button to add the word to the dictionary permanently.

Hot tip

If a field contains data that you know to be correct or that will confuse the spell-checker, such as a "surname" field, then click the "Ignore 'FieldName' Field" button. The spell-checker will then ignore that field in its entirety.

Formatting Data

Not only is an attractively styled database easy on the eye, styling can also be used to highlight items of importance. For example, we might apply a specific color to the data within a primary key field to denote it as such.

The Font Icon Group Explained

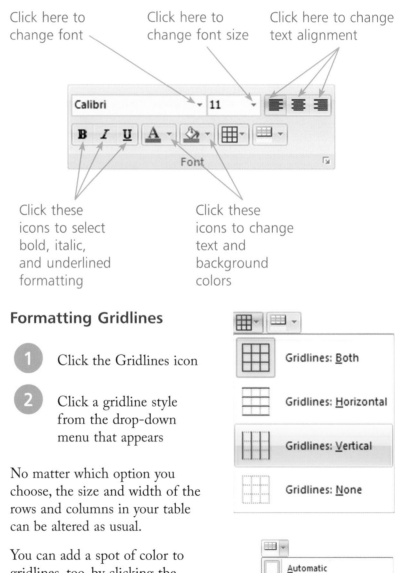

Click here to
change font

Click here to
change font size

Click here to change
text alignment

Click these
icons to select
bold, italic,
and underlined
formatting

Click these
icons to change
text and
background
colors

Formatting Gridlines

1 Click the Gridlines icon

2 Click a gridline style
from the drop-down
menu that appears

No matter which option you
choose, the size and width of the
rows and columns in your table
can be altered as usual.

You can add a spot of color to
gridlines, too, by clicking the
Gridline Color icon and selecting
a color from the menu.

Rich Text Formatting

New for Access 2007 is the ability to apply Rich Text Formatting to the Memo data type. Better still, the application of Rich Text Formatting to a Memo-based field can be viewed everywhere that the Memo field is used, whether it's in a table, a form, or a report.

You can format any cell within a memo-based field individually using either the Font icon group or the Rich Text icon group.

The Rich Text Icon Group Explained

Click here to decrease the list level

Click here to increase the list level

Click here to add a numbered list

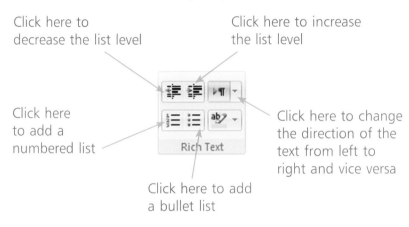

Click here to change the direction of the text from left to right and vice versa

Click here to add a bullet list

Hiding Columns

It is possible to hide columns from view temporarily. This is useful if you are working in a large table and don't want to enter data into all of the fields, as it allows you to see only the fields that are most important to you.

 Right-click the heading of the column you want to hide

Forename ▾	Surname ▾	DateOfBirth ▾	Salary ▾
Chris	Bones	11/8/1977	$15,000.00

 Choose Hide Columns from the context menu

Forename ▾	Surname ▾	Salary ▾
Chris	Bones	$15,000.00
William	Boorman	$20,000.00

Hot tip

Columns can also be hidden or unhidden by clicking the More icon in the Records icon group and clicking the appropriate entry in the drop-down menu.

...cont'd

Unhiding Columns

1 Right-click any field heading

2 Select Unhide Columns from the menu

3 Check the boxes of the fields you want to see

4 Click the Close button

Freezing Columns

Freezing a column ensures that it is always visible within that table window. This is useful if there is a field that you must constantly refer to during data entry, such as a name field.

1 Right-click the column you want to freeze

2 Select "Freeze Columns" from the context menu

To unfreeze a column simply click the heading of any field and select Unfreeze All Columns from the context menu.

Hot tip

Columns can also be frozen or unfrozen by clicking the More icon in the Records icon group and clicking the appropriate entry in the drop-down menu.

6 Querying Databases

A query is a set of instructions that specify criteria for selecting records. When executed, the query retrieves these records that satisfy the criteria. The process of creating queries isn't complicated, thanks to Access's powerful graphical interface.

What is a Query?

When you run a query you are asking Access to retrieve a set of records from one or more tables. The records are retrieved according to criteria that you, the user, provide. For example, consider the Books table below.

Books		
Title ▾	Author ▾	Price ▾
⊞ Throwing Hammers - A Retros	Ken Philips	$9.99
⊞ Stunning Creatures	Arthur Kent	$7.99
⊞ Crazy Mixed-Up Kids	Jimmy Scot	$7.99
⊞ King of Wishful Stinking	LM De'Pru	$7.99
⊞ Kane and Mabel	Jimmy Scot	$7.99
⊞ Craze the Pig Farmer	LM De'Pru	$7.99
⊞ Great Disappointments of the	Johannes Kipping	$29.99
⊞ Meadow Birds	Arthur Kent	$6.99

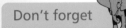

Don't forget

As can be seen, a query looks just like a table and for the most part behaves just like a table. You can even base a form or report on a query and use queries as the source tables for other queries.

Suppose we want to see only the records where the price of a book is $6.99. To do this we would create a "Select" query. The effects of running this Select query are shown below.

Budget Books		
Title ▾	Author ▾	Price ▾
Kane and Mabel	Jimmy Scot	$6.99
Meadow Birds	Arthur Kent	$6.99
Rave on, Monty!	Jimmy Scot	$6.99
What Doesn't Kill You	AJ Benedict	$6.99
Nursing Red Mercury	AJ Benedict	$6.99
Memoirs of a Superstar	Creole Williams	$6.99
Stunning Creatures	Arthur Kent	$6.99
Crazy Mixed-Up Kids	Jimmy Scot	$6.99
✳		

Although there are many different types of query, the Select query is the most commonly used. Other types of query include the Append query that adds new records to an existing table, the Delete query that permanently removes records from a table, and the Make Table query that, as its name suggests, makes a new table using the records it retrieves from other tables.

Using the Query Wizard

As with most things in Access, a fully functioning query can be created in a short space of time using a wizard. The wizard lets you choose between four different types of queries. The type we will create is the Select query.

 Click the Create tab

 Click the Query Wizard icon

Select the Simple Query Wizard option by clicking it

Click the OK button

 Select the table or query that you will use as the base for your query by using the drop-down menu

...cont'd

6 Use the arrow buttons in the center of the dialog to select the fields that will be displayed in your query, and then click the Next button

Simple Query Wizard

Which fields do you want in your query?

You can choose from more than one table or query.

Tables/Queries

Table: Books

Available Fields:

ISBN
Description

Selected Fields:

Title
Author
Price

> >> < <<

Cancel   < Back   Next >   Finish

If you've included a field that uses a Number-based data type you can have Access calculate the sum or average for that field. To do this, click the Summary radio button, and then click the Summary Options button.

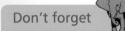

Simple Query Wizard

Would you like a detail or summary query?

○ Detail (shows every field of every record)

◉ Summary

Summary Options ...

1	aa	5
2	aa	7
3	cc	1
4	cc	8
5	ee	6

1	aa	12
2	cc	9
3	ee	6

Cancel   < Back   Next >   Finish

Check the boxes to have that function performed on a field.
When finished click the OK button and follow the steps below.

Don't forget

This will only appear
if you have included
Number-based fields in
your query.

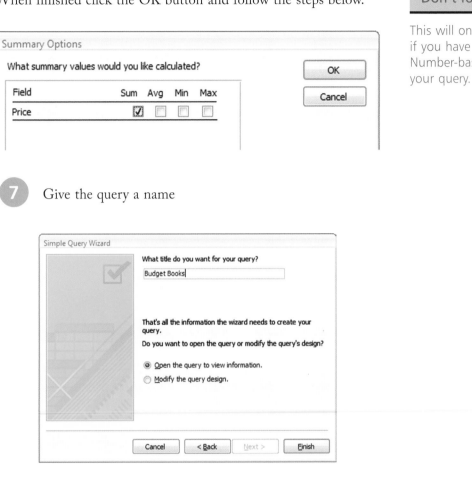

7   Give the query a name

8   Click Finish

The results of the query are presented as a table in Datasheet view.

Query Design View

Although the Query Wizard lets you choose only those fields that you want to see, it doesn't allow you to specify exacting criteria on which records should be selected. To create more advanced queries you'll need to use the Query Design view.

1 Click the Create tab

2 Click the Query Design icon

3 Double-click a table or query listed in the Show Table dialog to add it to the Query Design window

4 Click Close

5 Double-click a field name to add it to the query

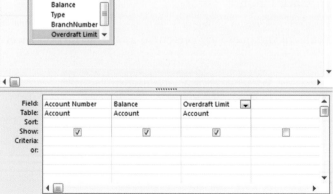

6 Add as many fields as you want to see in the final query

7 Click the Run icon on the Ribbon to use the query

The results are presented in a table.

Query1					✕
Account Nur ▾		**Balance ▾**		**Overdraft Limit ▾**	
100012		-£50.00		-£600.00	
100021		£581.00		-£50.00	
100023		£186.00		£0.00	
100043		£353,252.00		£0.00	
100045		£2,000.00		-£1,500.00	
100076		-£10,000.00		-£20,000.00	
100099		£1,000.00		£0.00	
*					

Saving a Query in Design View

Saving a query is much the same as saving a table.

1 Click the Save button in the Quick Access Toolbar

2 Type a name for the query in the Save As dialog

Save As	? ✕
Query Name:	
Accounts Overdrawn|	
	OK Cancel

> **Hot tip**
>
> You can also save a query by clicking the Office button and then clicking the Save option.

3 Click the OK button

Once saved, a query can be opened, executed, or modified whenever you want.

Adding Criteria to a Query

The most powerful feature of a query is its ability to select only those records that satisfy a particular condition. For example, we might want to view all the books in the Bobbin's Bookshop database that cost $6.99. To select records that satisfy this condition we can specify it in the Query Design window.

1 Create a query by following steps 1–6 on page 106

2 Click a cell on the Criteria row

Create a query by following steps 1–6 on page 106

Field:	Title	Author	Price	
Table:	Books	Books	Books	
Sort:				
Show:	☑	☑	☑	
Criteria:			=6.99	
or:				

Hot tip

Make sure you save the query if this is an operation you'll want to carry out in the future.

Hot tip

To retrieve all records where there is no value stored within a particular field, type "IS NULL" into the criteria field of the query design window.

3 Enter the condition that you want the query to satisfy

4 Click the Run Query icon

Run

5 The results are displayed in a table

Budget Books

Title	Author	Price
Kane and Mabel	Jimmy Scot	$6.99
Meadow Birds	Arthur Kent	$6.99
Rave on, Monty!	Jimmy Scot	$6.99
What Doesn't Kill You	AJ Benedict	$6.99
Nursing Red Mercury	AJ Benedict	$6.99
Memoirs of a Superstar	Creole Williams	$6.99
Stunning Creatures	Arthur Kent	$6.99
Crazy Mixed-Up Kids	Jimmy Scot	$6.99

Querying Multiple Tables

Queries can include fields drawn from a mixture of tables. It is also possible to specify criteria for more than one field in order to refine your query further. Suppose Bobbin's Bookshop wants to see which of the books written by Jimmy Scot were sold on 07/10/2008. We would need to use fields from both Sales and Books tables.

 Create a query by following the steps on page 106, adding as many tables as are necessary

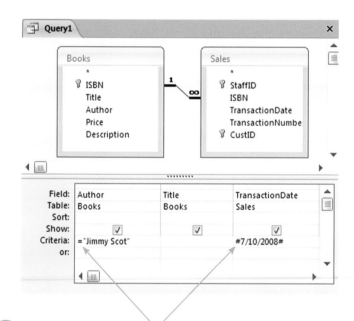

2 Specify the criteria you want to use in your query

3 Click the Run Query icon

4 The results are displayed in a table

Using Criteria for Numbers

A good understanding of how to specify criteria is key to creating an effective query. The more fluent you are in the use of criteria the more sophisticated and purposeful your queries will be.

The kind of criteria you use in a query depends on the data type of the fields to which you want to apply the criteria.

Criteria for Number Data Types

Perhaps the most useful of the criterion operators are the less than (<) and greater than (>) operators. They can be used either singly, to find all records where a value is greater than or less than another value, or together to restrict the records returned by the query to a specific range. For example, we might want to find all records in the Books table where the Price field contains a value greater than $7.00, as shown in the example below.

Field:	Author	Title	Price	
Table:	Books	Books	Books	
Sort:				
Show:	✓	✓	✓	
Criteria:			>7	
or:				

Alternatively, we might want to exclude a range of values. For example, Bobbin's Bookshop may want to retrieve all records in the Books table where a book is either priced under $7.00 *or* priced over $10.00. To specify such criteria we need to introduce the logical operators "and" and "or". An example is shown below.

Field:	Author	Title	Price	
Table:	Books	Books	Books	
Sort:				
Show:	✓	✓	✓	
Criteria:			<7 Or >10	
or:				

Finally, you can specify a range of values by using the word "between". For example, specifying the criterion "between 5 and 15" retrieves all those records containing a value that lies between those two numbers.

Hot tip

You can also use the greater than or equal to operator (>=) or the less than or equal to operator (<=).

Using Criteria for Text

The query criteria for number-based data types are designed to be specific in the values that are returned by a query that uses them. In contrast, query criteria for text-based data types are designed to retrieve more general results. This is to overcome the complexity of natural language and the problems that occur when a word entered into a table as a value has been misspelled.

For example, we might want to find all the records in the Books table of the Bobbin's Bookshop database where the Description field contains the word "crime". To do this we use the "Like" operator followed by a text string. An example is shown below.

Don't forget

A text string is simply a series of characters enclosed in speechmarks. For example, "I like Access" is a text string, as is "Queries make me euphorically happy".

Field:	Title	Author	Price	Description
Table:	Books	Books	Books	Books
Sort:				
Show:	☑	☑	☑	☑
Criteria:				Like "*crime*"
or:				

Notice how the word "crime" has an asterisk placed before and after it. The asterisk is known as the wildcard operator. In the example above it tells Access that anything before the word "crime" automatically satisfies the query criteria and that everything after it also satisfies the criteria. This is important because it means you can look for text strings that form *part* of a field's value rather than the whole.

The wildcard operator is useful if you only know part of a value and want to retrieve all the values that contain that part. For example, suppose we only know the first four letters of an employee's surname and want to search a table for the names of all employees whose surname begins with those first four letters. We would use the wildcard and "Like" operators again, as shown in the example below.

Field:	StaffID	Forename	Surname
Table:	Staff	Staff	Staff
Sort:			
Show:	☑	☑	☑
Criteria:			Like "Boor*"
or:			

Creating a Make Table Query

A Make Table query is a type of Action query that, when run, stores its results in a new table. A Make Table query is most useful for copying specific records that we want to look at in more detail. For example, suppose Bobbin's Bank want to have a separate table that only contains the details of accounts that are in excess of their overdraft limit. We could achieve this using a Make Table query.

1 Create a query following steps 1–6 on page 106

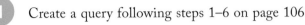

Field:	Account Number	Balance		Overdraft Limit
Table:	Account	Account		Account
Sort:				
Show:	☑	☑		☑
Criteria:		< = [Account].[Overdraft Limit]		
or:				

Don't forget

The Make Table icon can be found within the Query Type icon group, under the Design tab.

2 Enter any criteria you want to use in the query

3 Click the Make Table icon

4 Type a name for the new table in the Make Table dialog

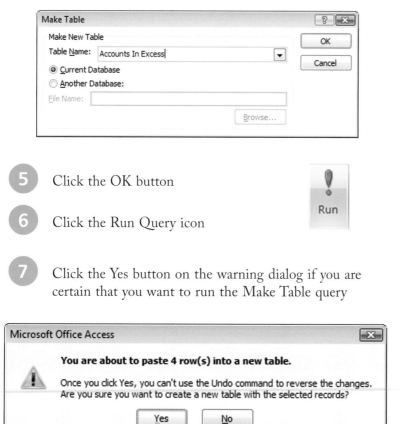

5 Click the OK button

6 Click the Run Query icon

Run

7 Click the Yes button on the warning dialog if you are certain that you want to run the Make Table query

Microsoft Office Access

You are about to paste 4 row(s) into a new table.

Once you click Yes, you can't use the Undo command to reverse the changes. Are you sure you want to create a new table with the selected records?

Yes   No

8 The newly created table appears in the Navigation Pane and can be opened and used like any other table

Accounts In Excess

Account Number	Balance	Overdraft Limit
100012	($750.00)	($600.00)
100021	($581.00)	($50.00)
100045	($2,000.00)	($1,500.00)
100076	($25,000.00)	($20,000.00)

Creating an Append Query

Beware

The effects of running an Append query are permanent and cannot be undone.

Don't forget

The Append icon can be found within the Query Type icon group, under the Design tab.

Hot tip

If the Append query is something you will use often then make sure you save it.

An Append query is an Action query that adds the selected records to another table. For example, suppose Bobbin's Bank wants to add accounts that have exceeded their overdraft limit to the Accounts in Excess table created on page 112. We could use an Append query to retrieve those accounts from the Accounts table and add them to the Accounts In Excess table.

1 Create a query following steps 1–6 on Page 106

2 Enter any criteria you want to use in the query

3 Click the Append icon

4 Choose a table to which to append the results of the query

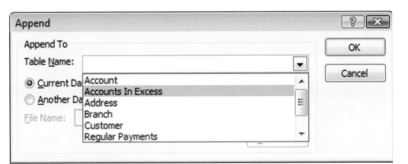

5 Click the OK button

6 Click the Run Query icon

7 Click the Yes button on the warning dialog if you are certain that you want to append the new rows

Microsoft Office Access	
⚠	**You are about to append 7 row(s).**
	Once you click Yes, you can't use the Undo command to reverse the changes. Are you sure you want to append the selected rows?
	Yes No

Creating an Update Query

An Update query is a type of Action query that updates records that already exist in a table. For example, suppose Bobbin's Bookshop want to change the price of all the $6.99 books to $7.99. Doing this manually would take a long time. It would be much quicker to use an Update query.

 1 Create a query following steps 1–6 on page 106

2 Enter any criteria you want to use in the query

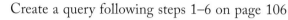

Query1   ✕

Books
- *
- ⚷ ISBN
- Title
- Author
- Price
- Description

Field:	Price		
Table:	Books		
Update To:	"7.99"		
Criteria:	=6.99		
or:			

115

3 Click the Update icon

Update

4 Enter new values into the "Update To" field

5 Click the Run Query icon

6 If you are certain you want to update the values click the Yes button on the warning dialog

Bobbin's Bookshop

⚠ **You are about to update 8 row(s).**

Once you click Yes, you can't use the Undo command to reverse the changes. Are you sure you want to update these records?

[Yes]   [No]

Creating a Delete Query

A Delete query is a type of action that permanently removes records from a table based on the criteria we specify. For example, suppose a customer wants their name to be removed from the Bobbin's Bookshop database.

1 Create a query by following steps 1–6 on page 106

2 Enter the criteria that will identify the records you want to delete

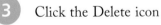

116

3 Click the Delete icon

4 Click the Run Query icon

5 If you are certain that you want to delete the records permanently click the Yes button on the warning dialog

7 Using SQL

SQL is a programming language that is used to create sophisticated queries. Although it may appear complex, learning the basics of SQL is surprisingly easy.

Using SQL

SQL is a programming language used exclusively within relational database management systems (referred to as DBMS for short), such as Access. By using SQL we can write code that can be used to retrieve data, modify data, and even create tables. However, SQL is most commonly used to write Select queries.

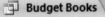

> **Budget Books** ✕
>
> SELECT Books.Title, Books.Author, Books.Price, Books.Description
> FROM Books
> WHERE Books.Price=6.99;

What is the point?
Given that Access is specifically designed to help users create databases without uttering a line of code, and that Microsoft have just spent untold millions making the user interface simpler than ever, you might be wondering why on earth anyone would want to play around with SQL.

The point is that not only can SQL be used with Access's native programming language Visual Basic for Applications, but it's also very easy to create sophisticated queries very quickly. Once you're used to SQL it's much quicker to type out a few lines of code for a Select query than to click your way manually through the graphical Query By Example system.

A Brief History of SQL
SQL was first conceived as a standard programming language for Relational Database Management Systems. At the time of its birth many different, competing languages were in use by different software vendors and usually each would only work with a particular database. Because of these differences, a business that had bought and implemented a database management system from one vendor then found it hard to migrate their existing database when a newer, better system from another vendor came along.

By adopting SQL as the standard database language, software companies found it easier to tempt customers away from their existing DBMS and customers were able to take advantage of cheaper or more efficient systems without too much disruption. A standard language also made it easier and faster for software engineers and programmers to implement their database designs.

The Three Languages of SQL

Although SQL is actually one language, it can be broken into three sub-languages containing statements specific to an area of database management.

Data Control Language (DCL)

The statements of this sub-language are used to administrate and secure databases. For example, they can be used to create new users or restrict what a user can do in a database.

However, Access does not support the use of Data Control Language statements in SQL View.

Data Definition Language

The statements in this sub-language can be used to create and alter the structure of a database. For example, they could be used to create, delete, or add fields to a table.

```
DDL Example                                    ×

CREATE TABLE Car (
RegNumber   text  NOT NULL,
Model  text   NOT NULL,
Color  Text  NOT NULL,
PRIMARY KEY (RegNumber));
```

Hot tip

To learn about SQL in greater detail be sure to read "SQL In Easy Steps".

Data Manipulation Language

This is the most commonly used group of statements in Access. They can be used to perform Select queries or modify data.

```
DML Example                                    ×

SELECT Books.Title, Books.Author, Books.Price, Books.Description,
Sales.TransactionDate
FROM Books INNER JOIN Sales ON Books.ISBN=Sales.ISBN
WHERE (((Sales.TransactionDate)=#7/10/2008#));
```

Throughout the rest of this chapter we'll be looking at how SQL can be used to create Select queries.

Opening the SQL Window

There are a few different ways to open the SQL window. First, open a query. This can be either an existing query or a query that you are in the process of designing.

Then click the Data Definition icon located in the Query Type icon group, under the Design tab.

Beware

Clicking the Data Definition button will cause Access 2007 to discard any unsaved queries you may have open in Design View.

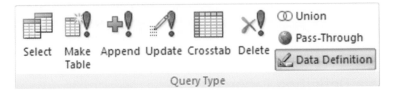

Or click the SQL icon at the foot of the main Access window.

> **SQL Select Query** ✕
>
> SELECT Author, Price
> FROM Books
> WHERE Price=6.99;

Alternatively, you can right-click the tab of a query window and select SQL View from the context menu.

> **Sales 07/10/2008**
>
> | | Save |
> | | Close |
> | | Close All |
> | | Design View |
> | SQL | SQL View |
> | | Datasheet View |
> | | PivotTable View |
> | | PivotChart View |
>
> Throw
> Stunni
> Crazy N
> King of
> Rave o
> Rave o
> Meado
> Meado
> Kane and Mabel

Using the SELECT Clause

The SELECT clause is the first element in a Select query to be written and is used to specify the fields that are displayed when the query is run.

At its most basic, the SELECT clause consists of the word "SELECT" followed by field names separated by commas, as in the example below.

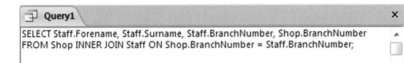
Staff Details

```
SELECT StaffID, Forename, Surname, DateOfBirth, Salary
FROM Staff;
```

When Select queries draw their information from more than one table it is necessary to distinguish fields with the name of the table they are selected from. This is done by linking a table name and a field by the period operator "." as in the example below.

Query1

```
SELECT Staff.Forename, Staff.Surname, Staff.BranchNumber, Shop.BranchNumber
FROM Shop INNER JOIN Staff ON Shop.BranchNumber = Staff.BranchNumber;
```

Sometimes a Select query can result in a table containing so many duplicate values that it can be difficult to interpret the results. For example, suppose Bobbin's Bookshop want to see the range of prices of the books they hold in stock. Running a simple Select query to retrieve the Price field from the Books table would result in a lot of duplicated prices because a value from the Price field would be retrieved from every record contained in the Books table. We can avoid this outcome by typing "DISTINCT" immediately after "SELECT".

Common Book Prices

```
SELECT DISTINCT Price
FROM Books;
```

Don't forget

To run an SQL query you need to click the Run Query icon, just as with any other query.

Run

121

Hot tip

To select all fields in a table write "SELECT *". When selecting fields from more than one table you'll need to specify the table name. For example, "SELECT Staff.*, Sales.*".

Don't forget

A Select statement must consist of at least two clauses: SELECT and FROM.

Using the WHERE Clause

The WHERE clause specifies the rows that are displayed when the query is run according to a condition. The condition could be a comparison of values using mathematical operators or it could be a logical comparison.

The following SQL statement uses the WHERE clause to select all the records from the Books table in the Bobbin's Bookshop database where the price of a book is $10.00 or over.

Books Over $10   ✕

```
SELECT *
FROM Books
WHERE [Books].[Price] >= 10.00
```

Suppose we wanted to be more specific and exclude all the books that are under $10.00 *and* all those written by Alan Carson. The following SQL code shows us how to do that.

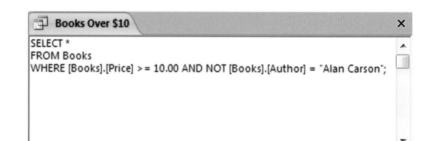

Books Over $10   ✕

```
SELECT *
FROM Books
WHERE [Books].[Price] >= 10.00 AND NOT [Books].[Author] = "Alan Carson";
```

The results of the above statement can be seen below.

Books Over $10

Title	Author	Price
Good Manners Cost Nothing	Lady Carrington-Smy	$12.99
An Historical Atlas of Mexico	Charles Gray	$14.99
Garden Parties Made Easy	Lady Carrington-Smy	$12.99
My Nightmare	Child Unknown	$14.99
Party Planning	Lady Carrington-Smy	$12.99
Charles, My Companion	Denver Rush	$14.99

SQL Aggregate Functions

Just like graphical queries SQL queries can also use aggregate functions such as COUNT() and SUM(). To use an aggregate function in SQL you need to specify it after the SELECT clause, as can be seen in the example below.

```
Query1                                                    ×
SELECT COUNT(TransactionNumber)
FROM Sales
WHERE TransactionDate = #07/10/2008#;
```

In this example, the SQL code above uses the COUNT function to find out how many transactions were made on the date 07/10/2008 by counting the number of entries in the TransactionNumber field. The image below shows the result.

```
Query1
  Expr1000      ▾
            14
```

The table below lists the most commonly used functions and explains their usage.

Function	Example Usage	Description
SUM()	SELECT SUM(FieldName) FROM TableName	Sums the values stored in a field
AVG()	SELECT AVG(FieldName) FROM TableName	Averages the values in a field
COUNT()	SELECT COUNT(FieldName) FROM TableName	Counts the records in a table that have a value in FieldName
MAX()	SELECT MAX(FieldName) FROM TableName	Finds the highest number in a field

123

Hot tip

The COUNT() function as described to the left only counts records that have a value in a particular field. To count every row in a table use the wildcard operator (*) in place of FieldName.

Creating Union Queries

A Union query is a type of SQL Select query that combines the records from two independent tables into one. The example below combines the Forename and Surname fields of the Customer table with the Forename and Surname fields of the Staff table.

1 Click the Design Query icon

2 Close the Show Tables dialog without adding any tables to the design

Union
Pass-Through
Data Definition

3 Click the Union icon

4 Type a SELECT statement for the first table that you want to include in the query

5 Type a second SELECT statement, typing UNION before the select clause

Union Query	×
SELECT Customer.Forename, Customer.Surname FROM Customer UNION SELECT Staff.Forename, Staff.Surname FROM Staff	

6 Click the Run Query icon

Union Query	
Forename ▾	**Surname** ▾
Ben	Atherton
Bill	Woodman
Chris	Jones
Gary	Hyman
Geoffrey	Aaron
Harriet	Lascelles
Jane	Lucas

(8) Creating Forms

Put simply, a form is a graphical interface between your users and Access. It "captures" the data supplied by a user and saves it to one or more tables. By using forms intelligently, you can improve the productivity of your users.

What is a Form?

An Access form is simply a window that invites users to enter information into your database. It is a graphical interface between your users and the database you have created.

By using forms in your database you will make data entry quicker and easier, and you'll improve the overall user experience.

Why Not Enter Data Directly into a Table?

Studies have shown that a well-designed user interface has a positive, beneficial effect on the people who use it. Apart from being easy on the eye, a well-designed interface makes efficient use of the screen space available and asks only for the specific information required to complete a given transaction.

You have to remember that some Access tables will contain lots of fields and lots of records. Even for someone familiar with such a table, updating and deleting the values in it will be a confusing and error-prone business. Given that, it would seem only reasonable for someone new to Access, when faced with such a table, to scream and exit the office through the window.

Designing the Perfect Form

Designing a form that pleases users and supports your business processes might take a bit of effort but it needn't be difficult. All you need to do is remember a few simple guidelines.

- Make the look and feel of your form consistent. Don't confuse users by suddenly changing the way they interact with your forms.

- Use words and terms that are familiar with, and appropriate to, your users. For example, if your business is based around selling books then refer to them on your form as "Books" and not "Products".

- Keep your forms clear and uncluttered. Don't add lots of controls or information onto your forms just because it looks good. This will scare users away.

- Thoroughly test your user interface. Make sure that all the controls on your form perform exactly as expected.

- Build your forms around the tasks that the users of your database will want to carry out.

Beware

If you don't provide a good interface for your database your users won't just make errors, they might even refuse to use it.

The Anatomy of a Form

A form on its own is pretty useless. It only becomes usable once we start adding controls to it, such as text boxes and buttons.

A control is an object that is designed to perform a particular function, such as taking input from a user or presenting a choice. Every control has a list of properties that dictate the way it looks and behaves. For example, changing a Label control's Font property will change the way the text displayed on it will look.

Controls can be divided into three different varieties: bound controls, unbound controls, and calculated controls.

Bound Controls

A bound control is linked directly to a field in a table or query. By changing the value in a bound control the user also changes the value in the table to which it relates. A good example of a bound control is the text box, pictured below.

Description: **The industry standard tome for all basket weavers, new or old, beginner or seasoned professional.**

Hot tip

For more information on controls and the types available see the training pages at Office Online.

Unbound Controls

An unbound control is not linked to any field, table or query. Often unbound controls are used to display information or to support the user interaction with a form. A good example of an unbound control is the command button, pictured below.

Calculated Controls

The value of a calculated control is based on a mathematical expression entered into the control's Record Source property. An example of a calculated control might be a text box that subtracts a percentage from the value in another field and then displays the results.

Throughout this chapter we'll look at each of the three types.

Using a Form for Data Entry

Data entry is the main purpose of a form. Because of that, Access 2007 provides a range of tools for navigating through records. These tools are included at the foot of nearly every form in the shape of five icons, shown below.

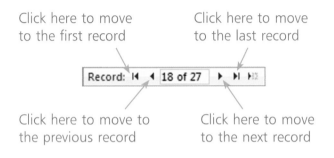

Click here to move to the first record

Click here to move to the last record

Record: 18 of 27

Click here to move to the previous record

Click here to move to the next record

The sequence of records is dictated by the order of the records in the underlying table or query upon which the form is based. The record at the top of a table will be the first one to be displayed and the record at the bottom of the table will be the last.

Adding a New Record

There are two methods of adding a new record to the underlying table or query upon which the form is based. The first method is to use a Ribbon icon.

1 Click the Home tab on the Ribbon

2 Click the New icon found within the Records icon group

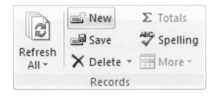

The second method is simply to click the New Record icon on the Record Navigation toolbar. This is the icon just to the right of the four discussed above.

Editing Data in a Form

Editing data in a form is as simple as editing data in a table.

 1 Click the text field of the value you want to edit

Title:	Stunning Creatures
Author:	Arthur Ke
Price:	$6.99

 2 Either delete the existing data and type a new value or amend the data that already exists

3 Press the Tab key to move to the next field

Deleting a Record

1 Navigate to the record you want to delete

2 Click the Home tab on the Ribbon

✕ Delete ▾
✕ **Delete**
⟝ **Delete Record**
⥮ Delete Column

 3 Click the down arrow to the right of the Delete icon to open the drop-down menu

4 Select Delete Record from the menu

5 Access now displays a warning. Click the Yes button if you are *sure* you want to delete the record

Microsoft Office Access	✕
⚠ **You are about to delete 1 record(s).**
If you click Yes, you won't be able to undo this Delete operation. Are you sure you want to delete these records?
[Yes] [No]

Hot tip

Press Shift+Tab to move to the previous field rather than the next.

Beware

The changes you make to a field will take effect the moment you press the Tab key to move into another field.

129

Beware

Deleting a record is not a reversible decision. Be certain that you want to delete a record before following these steps.

Filtering Forms

You may want to restrict the number of records a form can access according to some criteria. For example, suppose an employee of Bobbin's Bookshop only wants to view books that are priced at $6.99. We could do this by applying a filter to the form.

Filtering by Selection

1 Select the field that contains the criterion you want to use as the filter

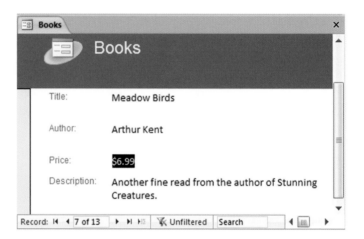

2 Click the Home tab on the Ribbon

3 Click the Selection icon and choose the most appropriate filter from the drop-down menu

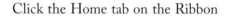

By looking at the status bar we can see that the filter has been applied. The number of records available will have been reduced and the Filtered button will be highlighted.

Hot tip

Press the Filtered button on the status bar to toggle the filter on or off. If you haven't set a filter in your current Access session, pressing the button will toggle the last filter that you previously used.

Applying a Detailed Filter

Sometimes it's handy to filter a range of values rather than limiting the filter to just one. For example, what if we wanted to access all the records in the Books table with prices of $6.99 and $7.99? To do this we'd need to apply a detailed filter.

 1 Click the text field that contains the data you want to filter

 2 Click the Home tab on the Ribbon

Filter

 3 Click the Filter icon. This can be found within the Sort & Filter icon group

 4 Select the criteria for the filter from the menu that appears below the text field you clicked earlier

A↓Z	Sort Smallest to Largest
Z↓A	Sort Largest to Smallest
🔻	Clear filter from Price:
	Number Filters ▶

☐ (Select All)
☐ (Blanks)
☑ $6.99
☑ $7.99
☐ $9.99
☐ $10.99
☐ $29.99

OK   Cancel

 5 Click the OK button to apply the filter

The number of records available will change accordingly.

Using the Form Wizard

The Form Wizard is a great means of creating a fully usable, attractive form remarkably quickly.

 Click the Create tab on the Ribbon

 Click the More Forms icon

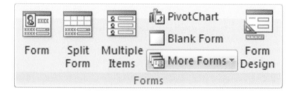

 Choose the Form Wizard icon from the menu

 Select the table or query upon which the form should be based, by using the drop-down menu

Hot tip

As the dialog states, you can select fields from different tables and queries. By using this feature you can build sophisticated forms that save you time by entering data into more than one table or query at once.

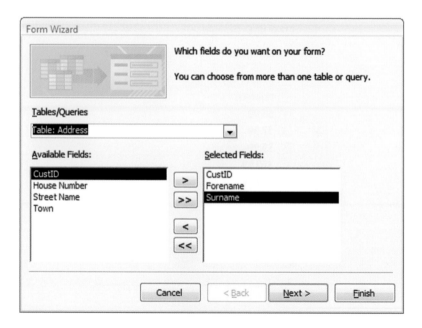

5 Use the arrows to select the fields that you want to appear in the form

132

6 Click the Next button

7 Click the radio buttons to choose a layout for the form

Form Wizard

What layout would you like for your form?

- ⦿ Columnar
- ○ Tabular
- ○ Datasheet
- ○ Justified

| Cancel | < Back | Next > | Finish |

8 Click the Next button

9 Highlight the style you want for your form

Form Wizard

What style would you like?

Label   Data

Access 2007
Apex
Aspect
Civic
Concourse
Equity
Flow
Foundry
Median
Metro
Module
None
Northwind
Office

| Cancel | < Back | Next > | Finish |

10 Click next

...cont'd

11 Type a title for your form here

> **Form Wizard**
>
> What title do you want for your form?
>
> Customer
>
> That's all the information the wizard needs to create your form.
>
> Do you want to open the form or modify the form's design?
>
> ◉ Open the form to view or enter information.
>
> ○ Modify the form's design.
>
> Cancel   < Back   Next >   Finish

12 Select this radio button if you want to open the form in Design View

13 Click the Finish button

Access opens the form in Form View ready for you to use.

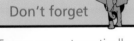

Don't forget

Forms are automatically saved and added to the Navigation Pane.

> **Customer**
>
> # Customer
>
> CustID   16
>
> Forename   Carlton
>
> Surname   Gregory
>
> House Number   47
>
> Street Name   Lister Park
>
> Town   Lawnceston
>
> Record: I◄ ◄ 2 of 2 ► ►I ►❏   No Filter   Search

Creating a Simple Form

You can have Access generate an attractive, fully usable form automatically in just a few easy steps.

 Click the Create tab on the Ribbon

Don't forget

When you click on the Form icon Access uses whatever table or query is highlighted in the Navigation Pane as the data source for the form.

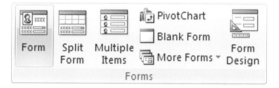

 Click the Form icon located within the Forms icon group

☷ Customer	✕

Customer

CustID:	5
Forename:	Luke
Surname:	Bennett
Sex:	Male

Record: ◄ ◄ 5 of 14 ► ►I ►☷   ☒ No Filter   Search   ◄ ►

 To enter data into the form click the Form View icon

Unlike those created by the Form Wizard, forms created by using the Form icon aren't automatically saved to the Navigation Pane. To keep the form you will need to save it manually.

Using Split Forms

A Split Form combines the easy data entry of a form with the versatility of a table in Datasheet View. Split Forms are incredibly useful when working with large tables or queries that contain a lot of entries or many fields. Users can quickly find the record they need to amend using the datasheet view of the table and use the form element of the Split Form to modify it.

Customer1			×

Customer

CustID: 1

Forename: Lee

Surname: Yates

CustID ▾	Forename ▾	Surname ▾
1	Lee	Yates
2	Ben	Atherton
3	Kyle	Green
4	Malcolm	Billings
5	Luke	Bennett

Record: ◄ 1 of 15 ► ►► ►⊞ ⅄ No Filter Search

Clicking a record in the datasheet portion of the window displays it in the form portion

Use the splitter bar to resize the datasheet and form portions of the window

Split Forms are much more than a novel means of data entry. Access provides Split Form specific properties that can be used to fine-tune your form, for example to alter the positioning of the datasheet element of the Split Form. The next two pages show you how to construct and modify a Split Form.

Creating a Split Form

 Highlight the table or query upon which the form will be based in the Navigation Pane

 Click the Create tab on the Ribbon

 Click the Split Form icon

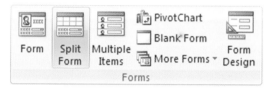

Fine-Tuning Split Forms

 Switch to Design View

 If the Property Sheet isn't already open, press the F4 key

 Click the drop-down menu to open it and then select "Form" from the list

All the Split Form specific properties can be accessed by clicking the Format tab on the Property Sheet. On the next page we'll see how they can be used to change the behavior of your Split Form.

...cont'd

Changing the Position of the Datasheet

The default position of the datasheet element of the Split Form is at the bottom of the form. However, this position won't suit all forms and it can be changed using the Split Form Orientation property as shown below.

Min Max Buttons	Both Enabled
Moveable	No
Split Form Size	Auto
Split Form Orientation	Datasheet on Bottom
Split Form Splitter Bar	Datasheet on Top
Split Form Datasheet	Datasheet on Bottom
Split Form Printing	Datasheet on Left
Save Splitter Bar Position	Datasheet on Right
Subdatasheet Expanded	No

Removing the Splitter Bar

After you've spent a long afternoon designing your Split Form with painstaking precision so that it looks just right on screen, you might then find yourself resenting users when they exercise a bit of free will and ruin your hard work by using the resize bar. To stop them from doing this you can completely remove it by using the Split Form Splitter Bar property.

Split Form Orientation	Datasheet on Bottom
Split Form Splitter Bar	No
Split Form Datasheet	Yes
Split Form Printing	No
Save Splitter Bar Position	Yes

Setting Datasheet Properties

To prevent users from making any careless mistakes when using the datasheet it's possible to make that portion of the Split Form window read-only. Users will still be able to locate a record using the datasheet but must use the form portion when entering or modifying data in a record. To make the datasheet read-only you need to alter the Split Form Datasheet property.

Split Form Splitter Bar	No
Split Form Datasheet	Read Only
Split Form Printing	Allow Edits
Save Splitter Bar Position	Read Only
Subdatasheet Expanded	No

Using Multiple Item Forms

The Multiple Items form takes its cue from the Datasheet View of a table or query, in that it displays many records on screen at the same time in a tabular format. However, it displays them in a more attractive and user-friendly manner.

 Click the Create tab on the Ribbon

 Click the Multiple Items icon

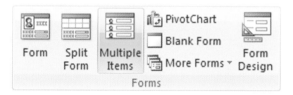

The form is displayed initially in layout view so that you can tweak elements as necessary. As with any other form, the design can be modified to suit your requirements.

Title	Author	Price
Kane and Mabel	Jimmy Scot	$6.99
Craze the Pig Farmer	LM De'Pru	$7.99
Meadow Birds	Arthur Kent	$6.99
Rave on, Monty!	Jimmy Scot	$6.99
What Doesn't Kill You	AJ Benedict	$6.99
Nursing Red Mercury	AJ Benedict	$6.99

Books

Record: ◄ ◄ 1 of 13 ► ►I ►⧉   ☒ No Filter   Search   ◄ ☐ ►

Finding a Record

With only one record in view on a form at any one time, having to find a specific record manually is an extremely tiresome task. Thankfully, Access 2007 gives us the Find icon, a handy search tool that lets us find records in a flash. It does so by searching a field for a specific data item.

The Find icon can be found under the Home tab within the Find icon group.

1 Click the text box of the field you want to search

2 Click the Find icon

3 Enter the value you are searching for in the "Find What" field of the Find and Replace dialog

Hot tip

You can also open the Find and Replace dialog by pressing the Ctrl+F keys simultaneously.

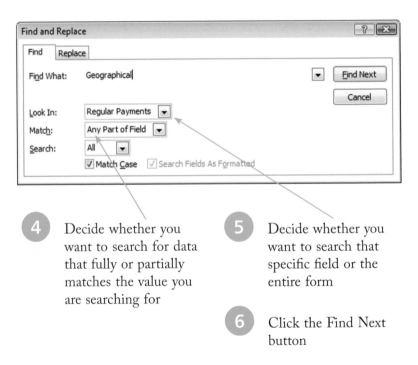

Hot tip

To find and replace one value with another, click the Replace tab. Enter the value you want to find in the Find What field and the value you want to replace it with in the Replace With field.

4 Decide whether you want to search for data that fully or partially matches the value you are searching for

5 Decide whether you want to search that specific field or the entire form

6 Click the Find Next button

It is highly likely that there will be more than one record that contains the value you entered. To cycle through them, continue pressing the Find Next button.

9 Fine-Tuning Forms

Although the wizards we saw in Chapter 8 are a great place to start the process of building truly spectacular user interfaces, you will need to fine-tune them to your exact specifications. In this chapter we see how you can add controls and macros to your forms to add greater functionality and automation.

Using Design View

Just as with the Design Views of the Table and Query database objects, the Form Design View offers you the opportunity to create a truly bespoke form from scratch or to fine-tune an existing form.

 Click the Create tab on the Ribbon

Click the Form Design icon. This can be found, rather predictably, in the Forms icon group

Form Design

Access opens a new form in Design View.

Elements of Design View

Use the ruler to fine-tune the positioning of form controls, such as a label

The Property Sheet lets you change the look and behavior of controls as well as the form itself

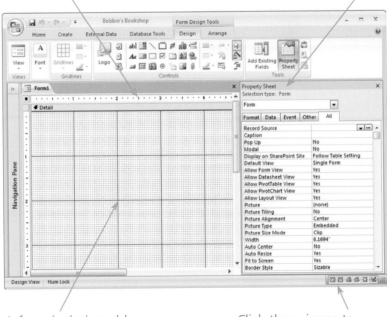

A form is designed by placing controls onto the Detail section

Click these icons to switch between different views of your form

Using Layout View

While Design View lets you produce forms with precision, you can't see exactly how a form will look until you "go live" with it. In previous versions of Access this meant switching between views to fine-tune controls, which was great until you switched to Form View and discovered that your lovingly crafted text fields weren't big enough for the data displayed in them!

Layout View is a halfway house between Design View and Form View. It allows you to make simple changes to the look and feel of a form, just as in Design View, yet it displays "live" data just as the regular Form View does.

Resizing Controls in Layout View

Beware

Although the Property Sheet and Field List can be used within Layout View, you may need to switch to Design View to make some changes.

1 Click on a control to select it. You'll know a control is selected because its outline turns orange

Account	×

Bobbin's Bank

Branch:	Carnation ▾
Account Number:	100012
CustID:	1
Balance:	-£750.00
Type:	Current ▾
BranchNumber:	131320
Overdraft Limit:	-£600.00

Record: I◄ ◄ 1 of 27 ► ►I ►⚹   No Filter   Search   ◄   III   ►

Hot tip

You can add existing fields to a form in Layout View using the Field List. This can be opened by pressing Alt+F8 or by clicking the Add Existing Fields icon.

2 Place the cursor at a corner of the orange outline. A double-headed arrow should appear

3 Click and hold down the left mouse button while dragging the mouse in the desired direction until the control is the right size and shape

Using the Field List

The Field List is a fast, efficient, and above all easy way of placing Text Fields and Labels onto a form. To use the Field List first open a form in either Layout View or Design View.

Opening the Field List

1 Click the Format tab on the Ribbon

2 Click the Add Existing Fields icon

The appearance of the Field List will vary depending on the number and type of relationships attached to the table that the form uses as its record source.

3 Click the plus sign to the left of a table name to see the fields contained in that table

4 Select a field to add to the form by clicking it and holding down the left mouse button

5 Drag the field to the form and then release the left mouse button

6 Repeat steps 1 to 5 until the form contains all the necessary fields

Field List

Fields available for this view:

⊟ Sales   Edit Table
    StaffID
    ISBN
    TransactionDate
    TransactionNumber
    CustID

Fields available in related tables:

⊞ Books   Edit Table
⊞ Customer   Edit Table
⊞ Staff   Edit Table

Fields available in other tables:

⊞ Address   Edit Table
⊞ FBS Sales Contacts   Edit Table
⊞ Shop   Edit Table
⊞ Stock List   Edit Table

Show only fields in the current record source

Adding Headers and Footers

A form is made up of different sections. Initially, when you create a form in Design View, only the Detail section is visible. This is because the Detail section is typically where you place the controls that transform your form from a blank page into something useful.

By using other sections, such as headers and footers, we can display information that isn't affected by changes within the Detail section of a form.

Viewing Headers and Footers

1 Right-click the Detail section of your form

2 Select the type of header you want to view from the context menu

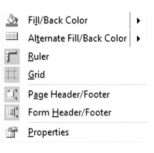

Form Headers and Footers

You would commonly use these sections to add corporate information, such as a logo, colors and name, as in the example from Bobbin's Bank below. The controls you place in the form header and footer can be seen on screen and in print.

Page Headers and Footers

These sections are only visible when you print a form or report. This might seem a bit pointless in the context of a form, but there are occasions when page headers and footers are useful. For example, suppose you create invoices using a form and then print off paper copies to send to customers. You could include contact information in the header that you would not ordinarily want to see when working with a form, such as an address or telephone number. You might even want to include your name and position together with a JPEG of your signature in the page footer.

Adding Controls to a Form

Although controls perform different functions and have unique properties that set them apart from one another, the process of adding them to a form is the same for all of them.

To add a control to a form first switch to Design View. The example below adds a label to a form.

1 Click the Design tab on the Ribbon

2 Select a control from the Control icon group by clicking its icon

3 Place the cursor at the position where you want the top left-hand corner of the control to be

4 Click and hold the left mouse button and then drag the cursor to the bottom-right

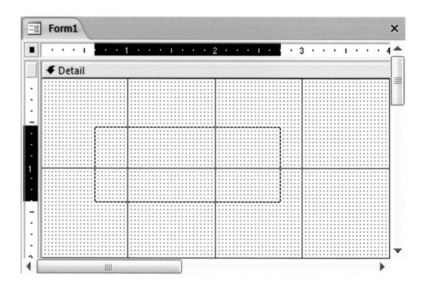

5 Use the ruler to help you set the right size for the control

6 Release the left mouse button

Fine-Tuning Controls

Resizing a Control

The ideal size of a control, whether it be a label, text box, or button, is dependent upon the size of the data that you want to put in it. Therefore, always check the sizing of a control when you have applied it to a form. If you find that you have made the control too big or too small you will need to resize it. To do this, click the control. You will see that the control is now bordered by an orange rectangle with eight protrusions sticking out of it.

The protrusions are, in fact, resize handles and are used to manipulate the size of the control. Click a resize handle with the

Don't forget

Check whether a control adequately contains your data by switching to Layout View, if necessary.

left mouse button and drag it in the desired direction, releasing the mouse button when the control is the correct size.

Don't forget

When you click a control it is said to have "focus".

Moving a Control

Click on a control so that it is bordered by an orange rectangle. Move the cursor to the top of the orange border. The cursor will become four arrow heads in a cross formation. Click and hold the left mouse button and move the control, releasing the mouse button when the control is at the desired position.

Attaching a Label to a Control

It is sometimes useful to have a control accompanied by a descriptive label so that users will understand its function. For example, a text box should always be accompanied by a label that indicates exactly what data should go into it.

1. Create a label

2. Click the Cut icon on the Clipboard icon group

3. Click the control you want to attach the label to

4. Click the Paste icon, also on the Clipboard icon group

Changing Control Properties

Every control, including the form itself, has a set of properties associated with it. By changing these properties we can tailor a control to our specific needs. For example, we might want to make the text on a button blue rather than the default black. Or we might want to change the font type and size of the text on a label.

Control properties can be changed in either Layout View or Design View using the Property Sheet. To open the Property Sheet in Design View, click the Design tab on the Ribbon and then click the Property Sheet icon located within the Tools icon group. In Layout View the Property Sheet can be found under the Arrange tab within the Tools icon group.

Changing a Property

Hot tip

You can also open the Property Sheet by pressing the F4 key.

1 Use the drop-down menu at the top of the Property Sheet to select the control you want to amend

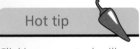

Hot tip

Clicking a control will change the focus of the Property Sheet to that control, so that you can alter its properties.

2 Select the property to amend, by clicking its value

Most properties are changed using a drop-down menu as in the example to the right, but sometimes you might see an ellipsis "..." icon. Clicking this icon will usually start a wizard that will guide you through the process of changing the value of that property.

Property Sheet		×
Selection type: Command Button		
A Button	▼	
A Button		
Auto_Title0		
Detail		
Form		
FormFooter		
FormHeader		
Visible	Yes	
Cursor On Hover	Default	
Picture	(none)	
Picture Type	Embedded	
Width	2.0833"	
Height	0.9167"	
Top	1.5833"	
Left	1.3333"	
Back Style	Normal	
Transparent	No	▼
Font Name	Calibri	
Font Size	11	
Alignment	Center	
Font Weight	Normal	
Font Underline	No	
Font Italic	No	
Fore Color	#00B7EF	
Hyperlink Address		
Hyperlink SubAddress		
Gridline Style Top	Transparent	
Gridline Style Bottom	Transparent	
Gridline Style Left	Transparent	
Gridline Style Right	Transparent	
Gridline Color	#000000	
Gridline Width Top	1 pt	
Gridline Width Bottom	1 pt	
Gridline Width Left	1 pt	
Gridline Width Right	1 pt	
Top Padding	0.0208"	

Control properties are grouped by function under the tabs at the top of the Property Sheet.

Creating Calculated Controls

Creating a Calculated Control

A calculated control gets its value from an expression entered into its Control Source property. The example below describes the process of adding a calculated control to a form.

Suppose Bobbin's Bookshop are running a promotion that entitles every customer to 20% off their purchase. Rather than have the cashier work out the resulting price it makes much more sense to have the form do it for us.

 1 Switch the form to Design View

2 If you have not already done so, add a text box to the form to display your calculations

3 If the Property Sheet is not already open, then open it now by pressing the F4 key

4 Click the Data tab on the Property Sheet

Format	Data	Event	Other	All
Control Source		= [Price]-[Price]*0.2	⬇ ...	
Text Format		Plain Text		

5 Click the Control Source property and enter the expression you want calculated

6 Switch back to Form View to check that the field displays the result you expect

Price:	$10.99
Promotional Price:	$8.79
Description:	The industry standard tome for all basket weavers whether new or old, beginner or seasoned professional.

Beware

Do not use a text box added to a form with the Field List as the basis for a calculated control, as some of its properties will have been set elsewhere. This means that the control might not function as intended and it might not be obvious which property is causing the problem.

149

Hot tip

If you are calculating a price or some other currency value, as in this example, remember to set the Format property of the text box to Currency.

Changing Tab Order

Just as pressing the Tab key in a table's Datasheet View moves the cursor from cell to cell, pressing the Tab key while using a form shifts focus from control to control. By default Access "tabs" between controls in a left to right, top to bottom fashion, but this might not be appropriate for every form that you create.

If this is the case, you can change the order in which users "tab" between controls by switching the form to Design View, clicking the Arrange tab on the Ribbon, and then clicking the Tab Order icon within the Control Layout icon group.

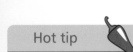

Hot tip

If you want to restore the controls to the default tab order, click the Auto Order button on the Tab Order dialog.

150

1 Choose between sections by clicking here

2 Select a control to move by clicking and holding down the left mouse button here

Tab Order

Section:

Form Header
Detail
Form Footer

Custom Order:

ISBN
Title
Author
Price
Description
Next Record
Previous Record

Click to select a row, or click and drag to select multiple rows. Drag selected row(s) to move them to desired tab order.

OK   Cancel   Auto Order

3 Still holding down the left mouse button, drag the control name to the desired position in the tab order

4 Repeat steps 1–3 until all the controls in your form are in the desired order

Creating a Tabbed Form

The tab control makes it easy to organize information from different sources into a logical order, all within the same control. A good example of the way tabs can be used to organize information and objects is the Ribbon you use to access command icons.

A form with a tab control is more formally referred to as a multi-page form, with each tab representing one page.

Adding a Tab Control to a Form
Before you add a tab control to a form make sure that you have the form open in Design View.

 Click the Design tab on the Ribbon

 Click the Tab Control icon

 Double-click the left mouse button at the point where you want the tab control to be placed

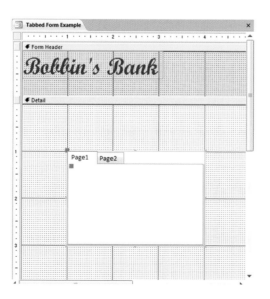

Hot tip

Use command buttons instead of tabs to change pages by setting the Style property of the tab control to Buttons.

Hot tip

It is possible to have more than one row of tabs on a tab control. To enable multiple rows of tabs select the tab control within the Property Sheet and set the Multi Row property to "yes".

...cont'd

Adding More Tabs

1	Right-click a tab
2	Select "Insert Page" from the context menu

Organizing Tabs

1	Right-click a tab
2	Select "Page Order..." from the context menu
3	Highlight the page you want to move by clicking it

Hot tip

Delete tabs by right-clicking the tab you want to remove and selecting "Delete Page" from the context menu.

Build <u>E</u>vent...

✂ Cut

🗍 <u>C</u>opy

🗋 <u>P</u>aste

Insert Page

Delete Page

Page <u>O</u>rder...

Ta<u>b</u> Order...

<u>A</u>lign ▶

<u>S</u>ize ▶

Properties

Page Order ? ✕

Page Order:

Page 12
Page 13
Page 14
Page 15
Page 16
Page 17

OK

Cancel

Move <u>U</u>p

Move <u>D</u>own

4	Click the "Move Up" or "Move Down" button to change the order in which the tabs are organized
5	Click the OK Button

Adding Controls to a Page

A tab control isn't particularly useful unless you have something to display on it. In the example below we're going to add a button to each page, but these could just as easily be other controls. It's even possible to have a Datasheet View of a table on each page!

 Decide which page you want to add the control to and click its tab

2 Choose a control from the Controls icon group by clicking its icon

3 Place the control within the orange border of the page

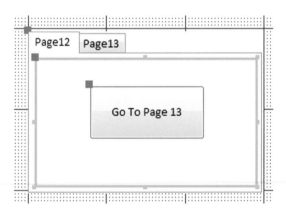

Don't forget

To ensure that you are applying a control to the right page check that the page is selected in the Property Sheet.

153

4 Click the tab of the next page

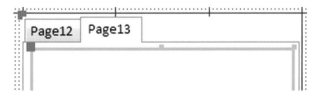

5 Add a control within the orange border of this page

6 Repeat the above steps for any other pages

Using Buttons

Buttons are possibly the most versatile of all form controls. They can be used to open database objects, switch views, or support a variety of data entry tasks. In the example below we will add a button to a form and use the Command Button Wizard to assign some functionality to it.

1 Switch the form to Design View

2 Click the Design tab on the Ribbon

3 Click the Button icon

ab|	Aa	xxxx
Text Box	Label	Button

4 Apply the button to the form

5 Once you've applied the button to the form Access opens the Command Button Wizard. Decide which action you want to assign to the button by clicking a category

---

Command Button Wizard

Sample:

▶

What action do you want to happen when the button is pressed?

Different actions are available for each category.

Categories:	Actions:
Record Navigation	Find Next
Record Operations	Find Record
Form Operations	Go To First Record
Report Operations	Go To Last Record
Application	Go To Next Record
Miscellaneous	Go To Previous Record

Cancel | < Back | Next > | Finish

---

6 Then click the action you want the button to perform

7 Click the Next button

8 If you want the button to display text click here

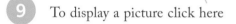

Command Button Wizard

Sample:

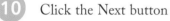

Do you want text or a picture on the button?

If you choose Text, you can type the text to display. If you choose Picture, you can click Browse to find a picture to display.

- ○ Text: Next Record
- ◉ Picture: Arrow Right
-           Go To Next   Browse...

☐ Show All Pictures

Cancel   < Back   Next >   Finish

Hot tip

You can preview how your button will appear by looking at the "Sample" pane at the left of the dialog. Every time you click a picture it is updated.

9 To display a picture click here

10 Click the Next button

11 Finally, type a name for your button

12 Click the Finish button

Hot tip

If you have designed your own icon for the button you are creating you can add it by clicking the "Browse" button. Use the File Dialog that opens to navigate to the icon you want to use.

Command Button Wizard

Sample:

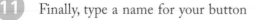

What do you want to name the button?

A meaningful name will help you to refer to the button later.

Button_NextRecord

That's all the information the wizard needs to create your command button. Note: This wizard creates embedded macros that cannot run or be edited in Access 2003 and earlier versions.

Cancel   < Back   Next >   Finish

Creating a Modal Dialog

The name might be unfamiliar but you'll certainly have come across a modal dialog before. It's a screen that either informs you of some impending danger or demands a "yes" or "no" response before letting you continue. No matter how hard you try, you won't be able to use Access until you've pressed a button on the dialog. Modal dialogs are particularly good at saving users from themselves. For example, we might want to warn a user that carrying out an Update Query will permanently alter existing records. In the example below the modal dialog asks users whether they're certain they want to close a database.

1 Click the More Forms icon

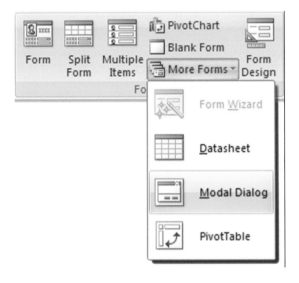

2 Select Modal Dialog from the drop-down list

3 Access opens the modal dialog in Design View.

In its initial state a modal dialog isn't very useful. Switching to Form View and pressing the "OK" and "Cancel" buttons achieves little other than letting you carry on using Access. To give it meaning, we must add a label stating the purpose of the dialog.

4 Click the Design tab on the Ribbon

5 Click the Label icon located in the Controls icon group

6 Move the cursor to the point on the form where you want the label to be placed

7 Hold down the left mouse button and drag the mouse to the bottom right of the form until you've created a rectangle big enough to display the label

8 Type a message into the label

Form1	✕

Are you sure you want to exit this application?

OK   Cancel

Chances are that when you create a modal dialog you'll want the buttons on the form to say something more descriptive than "OK" and "Cancel", and do something more useful than closing the dialog. In the next few steps we'll change the label on the dialog and attach a macro to a button that will close Access completely.

...cont'd

9 Click the "OK" button

10 If need be, change the Caption property for the button

11 Click the "Event" tab on the property sheet

Property Sheet				✕
Selection type: Command Button				
Command1				▾
Format	Data	Event	Other	All
On Click			[Embedded Macro] ▾ ···	▲
On Got Focus				
On Lost Focus				

12 Click the "..." button at the right of an event property. The most obvious event to use in the context of a button is "On Click"

Form1 : Command1 : On Click			✕
Action	Arguments	Comment	
CloseDatabase ▾			
CancelEvent			
ClearMacroError			
Close			
CloseDatabase			
FindNext			
FindRecord			
GoToControl			
GoToPage			
GoToRecord		Action Arguments	
Hourglass			
LockNavigationPane			
Maximize			
Minimize			
MoveSize		Closes the current database.	
MsgBox			
NavigateTo			

Hot tip

More information about macros is on page 160.

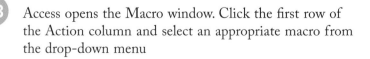

13 Access opens the Macro window. Click the first row of the Action column and select an appropriate macro from the drop-down menu

14 Click the Close icon

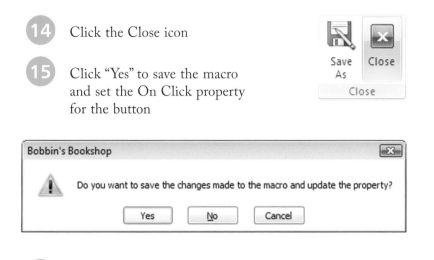

15 Click "Yes" to save the macro and set the On Click property for the button

Bobbin's Bookshop

⚠ Do you want to save the changes made to the macro and update the property?

Yes   No   Cancel

16 Click the Save icon on the Quick Access Toolbar

17 Type a name for the form

18 Click OK

The form is now ready to use and include in your applications.

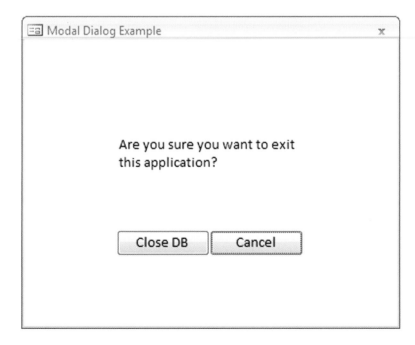

Using Macros

A macro is a set of actions that, when executed, perform some function, such as opening a form or running a query. They are most commonly used in association with forms where they run in response to some event triggered by the user, such as the click of a button or the movement of a mouse over an object.

Creating a Macro

1 Click the Create tab on the Ribbon

2 Click the Macro icon in the Other icon group

3 Click the Action column and choose an action to be performed from the drop-down menu

4 Click the Run icon

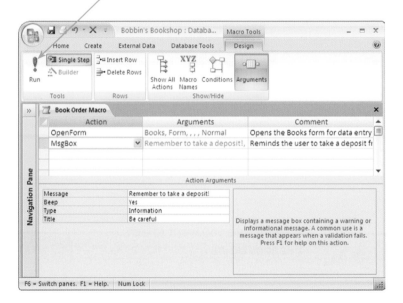

At the foot of the Macro screen you'll find the Action Arguments pane. Here you can provide information to the macro to help it perform the required function. For example, the image above shows the arguments given to the MsgBox action. They tell Access to display a message box containing the text in the Message argument.

Beware

Macros are powerful and can damage or delete the data in your database if you use them carelessly. Make sure you fully understand the consequences of running an action before you include it in a macro.

Hot tip

Macros are mini-programs. By combining them sequentially you can automate mundane activities such as creating and opening reports.

Hot tip

Use the Comment field to describe the purpose of the macro. Although it might seem obvious to you now it won't in six months' time!

10 Creating Reports

Reports unlock the information in your Access database and plant it firmly on the printed page. Once there, you can use that information to influence decision-making in your favor or demonstrate the success of your business. Alternatively, you may just want to print labels!

Using the Report Wizard

The quickest way to produce an attractive, professional-quality report is to use the Report Wizard.

1 Click the Create tab on the Ribbon

2 Click the Report Wizard icon

3 In the Report Wizard dialog, select the table or query you want to base the report upon from this drop-down menu

Hot tip

You can include fields from more than one table or query.

Report Wizard

Which fields do you want on your report?

You can choose from more than one table or query.

Tables/Queries

Table: Books

Available Fields:

ISBN
Price

Selected Fields:

Title
Author
Description

Cancel   < Back   Next >   Finish

4 Select the fields to include in the report by clicking the top two arrow icons

5 Click the Next button

6 Use the arrow icons to add grouping levels

Report Wizard

Do you want to add any grouping levels?

Author
Title, Description

Title

> <
⬆
Priority
⬇

Grouping Options ...   Cancel   < Back   Next >   Finish

Hot tip

If you have more than one grouping level you can use the Priority icons, shown to organize the grouping.

Hot tip

Click the Grouping Options button to set the grouping interval.

7 When you've finished, click the Next button

8 Dictate the sort order for the report using the drop-down menu. You can select up to four fields to sort upon

Report Wizard

What sort order do you want for detail records?

You can sort records by up to four fields, in either ascending or descending order.

1	Title	▾	Ascending
2		▾	Descending
3		▾	Ascending
4		▾	Ascending

Cancel   < Back   Next >   Finish

9 Click the Next button

...cont'd

10 Use this screen to decide upon the layout of your report by clicking these radio buttons

11 Choose the page orientation for the report by clicking the radio buttons. For reports containing many fields it's probably best to choose Landscape

12 Click the Next button to continue

13 Use this screen to choose the theme for your report

14 Click the Next button to continue

15 Type a title for the report here

Report Wizard

What title do you want for your report?

Books1

That's all the information the wizard needs to create your report.

Do you want to preview the report or modify the report's design?

○ Preview the report.

○ Modify the report's design.

| Cancel | < Back | Next > | Finish |

16 Choose between opening the report and modifying it in Design View by clicking the radio buttons

17 Click the Finish button to complete the wizard

Books1

Bobbin's Book Catalog

Author	Title	Description
AJ Benedict		
	Nursing Red Mercury	
	What Doesn't Kill You	
Arthur Kent		
	Meadow Birds	Another fine read from the author of Stunning Creatures.
	Stunning Creatures	A polished, if somewhat slight, encyclopedia of the rare and exotic fauna that stroll about this planet. Highlights include a breathtaking series of images of the lesser-spotted leopard.
Creole Williams		
	Memoirs of a Superstar	

Page: 1   Unfiltered

Creating a Simple Report

You can have Access 2007 create an attractive report from scratch in just a few easy steps.

1 Click the Create tab on the Ribbon

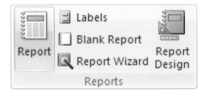

2 Click the Report icon

Once you've created a report, remember to save it by clicking the Save icon on the Quick Access Toolbar or by pressing the Ctrl+S keys simultaneously.

Title	Author	Description
Kane and Mabel	Jimmy Scot	
Great Disappointments of the 20th Century	Johannes Kipping	Everyone always goes on about the achievements of the 20th Century. Here, Johannes Kipping redresses the balance to good effect.
Craze the Corinthian	LM De'Pru	
Meadow Birds	Arthur Kent	Another fine read from the author of Stunning Creatures.
Rave on, Monty!	Jimmy Scot	A Rite Of Passage tale set in the hedonistic, drug fuelled London of the early nineties. A must for the nostalgic.
What Doesn't Kill You	AJ Benedict	
Nursing Red Mercury	AJ Benedict	
Memoirs of a Superstar	Creole Williams	
Weaving Baskets The Professional Way	Mariella Faux	The industry standard tome for all basket weavers, new or old, beginner or seasoned professional.
Throwing Hammers - A Retrospective	Ken Philips	A pictorial wander down memory lane focusing on the quaint sport of Hammer Throwing. The narrative, although heavily

Bobbin's Book Catalog — 7:50:32 PM

Access opens the report into Layout View for fine-tuning. Use the icons at the base of the report to switch between views.

Report View   Print Preview   Layout View   Design View

Using Report Design View

Creating a report in Design View gives you the ultimate creative freedom to present your data exactly as you need it. The process of fashioning a report in Design View is pretty much the same as that of fashioning a form in Design View (see page 142). All the same controls are at your disposal and you have recourse to the Property Sheet and Field List, just as in the form Design View.

The main difference is that the end product of using Report Design View is intended for the printed page and for that reason the icon groups available to the report designer are specifically geared towards page layout.

Creating a Report in Design View

1 Click the Create tab on the Ribbon

2 Click the Report Design icon located within the Reports icon group

The icons within the Arrange tab enable you to align your controls correctly, order the layout of your controls, and layer your controls and images

Use the icons within the Page Setup tab to adjust the page orientation, margins, and columns of your report

Don't forget

Once you've created a report remember to save it by clicking the Save icon on the Quick Access Toolbar or by pressing the Ctrl+S keys simultaneously.

167

Hot tip

To add a bit of originality to your report, click the Arrange tab and then click the AutoFormat icon. Choose a theme for your report from the drop-down menu.

Adding Fields to a Report

When you need to create a report in a hurry the Field List is indispensable. By clicking a few field names in the Field List you can have the bare bones of a report set up in minutes – giving you the time to concentrate on the appearance of the report so that you can present your data in the best light possible.

1 Open a report in either Layout View or Design View

2 Click the Add Existing Fields icon

3 Expand the plus symbol next to the name of the table you want to use

4 Double-click the names of the fields you want to add to the report

As can be seen from the image to the right, it is possible to add fields from both related and unrelated tables.

The field headings will appear in the Page Header of the report while the text boxes holding the data itself will appear in the Detail section, as can be seen in the image below.

Logo   Add Existing Fields

Controls

Field List	×
Fields available for this view:	
⊟ Books	Edit Table
ISBN	
Title	
Author	
Price	
Description	
Fields available in related tables:	
⊟ Sales	Edit Table
StaffID	
ISBN	
TransactionDate	
TransactionNumber	
CustID	
Fields available in other tables:	
⊞ Address	Edit Table
⊞ Customer	Edit Table
⊞ FBS Sales Contacts	Edit Table

Report1

Page Header					
ISBN	Title	Author	Price	Description	
Detail					
ISBN	Title	Author	Price	Description	
Page Footer					

Adding Controls to a Report

Adding a control to a report is much the same process as adding a control to a form.

 Switch to Design View

 Click the Design tab and select a control from within the Controls icon group

3 Click the point on the report where you want the top-left corner of the control to be positioned

4 Keep the left mouse button depressed while you drag the cursor to the bottom left

5 Let go of the left mouse button to place the control

6 Adjust the properties of the control to suit your needs by using the Property Sheet

Resizing a Control on a Report

First, click a control to select it. You will know that a control is selected because it will gain an orange border as shown in the image below. Also visible in the image below are eight protrusions, located at each corner and each edge of the control. These are resize handles. Click a resize handle, keep the mouse button depressed, and move the cursor in the direction that the resize handle faces to resize the control.

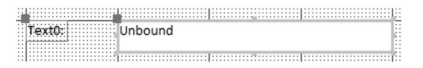

Hot tip

To open the Property Sheet without first traversing a thousand icons, press the F4 key.

Adding Headers and Footers

 1 Right-click the report

 2 Select Page Header/
Footer or Report
Header/Footer from
the context menu that
is displayed

🎨	Fi**ll**/Back Color ▶
▦	Al**t**ernate Fill/Back Color ▶
📏	**R**uler
▦	**G**rid
✖	Toolbox
🗋	P**a**ge Header/Footer
▤	Report **H**eader/Footer
🖼	**P**roperties

The report headers and footers define a structure for the report. This structure aids the creation of a report by dictating what report elements and controls go where. In this topic we'll look at the different types of headers and footers and provide examples of how they should be used.

The Report Header
This section will appear only once on a printed report and for that reason is best suited to titles, logos, contact details, and so on.

The Page Header
Controls and design elements placed in this section will appear at the top of every printed page. The page header is therefore best suited to column headings.

The Page Footer
This section appears at the bottom of every printed page. Use this section for page numbers, dates, author name, et cetera.

The Report Footer
Use this section for displaying totals and summary information.

Sorting and Grouping Data

Grouping and sorting the data in a report helps you to make sense of your data more easily. For example, suppose Bobbin's Bookshop want to create a report where data is grouped using an author's name with the titles of that author's books sorted from A to Z. The example below shows how this can be done.

1 Switch the report to Layout View or Design View

2 Click the Group & Sort icon

3 The Group, Sort, and Total pane opens at the base of the main Access window. This shows the current grouping and sorting structure of the report. If there is no grouping in the report click the "Add a group" button

4 Select the field you want to use for grouping data from the menu, by clicking it

5 To sort data within the group, click the "Add a sort" button

6 Choose a field upon which to sort the data from the menu

By using the Group, Sort, and Total pane you can create up to ten grouping levels. If you would prefer to group data on an expression rather than a field, click the Expression menu item at step 6 rather than a field name.

Printing Labels

Of the many features to support business processes in Access 2007, perhaps the most useful is the mailing label wizard. As well as doing the obvious and printing data to sticky labels for a mailshot, the label wizard is also handy for making visitor passes or stickers for customer files. Once you've generated the label report you can amend it to your needs – just like any other report.

1 Find the product code for your labels on their packaging and make a note of it

2 Use the Navigation Pane to open the table or query that contains the data for your labels

3 Click the Create tab on the Ribbon

4 Click the Labels icon. This can be found in the Reports icon group

5 In the Label Wizard dialog that opens up, use the Filter By Manufacturer drop-down menu to specify the brand of your labels

6 Select the unit of measurement that applies to your labels by clicking the relevant radio button

Beware

If you're wondering why your labels aren't printing properly be sure to check that you've specified the correct unit of measurement for your labels. Many manufacturers use the same product code for their English and metric labels, which can lead to a lot of confusion!

Label Wizard

This wizard creates standard labels or custom labels.

What label size would you like?

Product number:	Dimensions:	Number across:
L2163 (½ sheet)	50.8 mm x 101.6 mm	1
L2164 (½ sheet)	14 mm x 50 mm	2
L2186 (½ sheet)	50.8 mm x 69.85 mm	1
Avery J8159	64.0 x 33.9 mm	3
Avery J8160	63.5 x 38.1 mm	3

Unit of Measure
○ English ● Metric

Label Type
● Sheet feed ○ Continuous

Filter by manufacturer: Avery

Customize...   ☐ Show custom label sizes

Cancel   < Back   Next >   Finish

7 Click the product code that matches your labels, using the scrollbars if necessary

8 Click the Next button

9 Use the drop-down menus to select the font that will be used for your labels

10 Click the Next button

Hot tip

The image at the left of the dialog is updated to reflect the formatting choices you have made.

11 Click a field to highlight it and then click the arrow icon to add it to the prototype label

Don't forget

Remember to add a space between fields! To start a new line, press the Return key.

Don't forget

Remember that you can type free text into the prototype label, which could be handy if you want to include a brief message or note.

12 Repeat step 11 until the prototype label is complete

...cont'd

 Click the Next button to continue

 Your labels can be sorted on one or more fields; for example, you might want your address labels sorted by surname or town

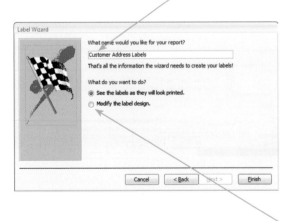

Click the Next button to continue

Type a name for your report here

Decide between opening the report to print or opening it in Design View

 Click the Finish button

Setting Custom Label Sizes

If you happen to have come across your labels while raiding the deepest recesses of your predecessor's filing cabinet and it appears that the product code is but a long-distant memory, don't panic. It's still possible to make use of them.

1 Open the Label Wizard dialog by following steps 1 to 4 on page 172

2 On the first screen of the Label Wizard dialog, click the Customize button

3 This launches the New Label Size dialog. Click the New button to launch the New Label dialog

4 In the lower half of the dialog are a series of rectangles containing the values "0.00" next to double-headed arrows. These correspond to a particular dimension of the label. Click a rectangle and then enter the correct value for your set of labels.

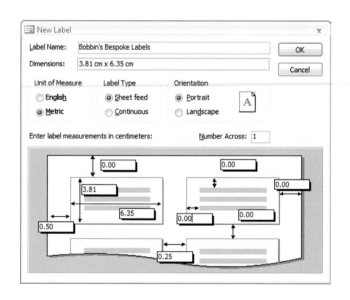

Don't forget

Make sure you specify the correct unit of measure for your labels.

Don't forget

Remember to input a name for your labels.

5 Repeat step 4 until all measurements have been entered

6 Click the OK button

Using Print Preview

Print Preview is much more than a means of looking at a report before it is sent to print. In Print Preview mode it's possible to set the margins of a report, split a report into two or more columns, and export the report to other applications.

Switching to Print Preview

There are three ways of switching to Print Preview mode.

The simplest way is to click the View icon on the Ribbon and select Print Preview from the drop-down menu.

The second method is to use the Print Preview icon at the base of the report window, as shown on page 166.

The final method of switching to Print Preview is by using the Office Button.

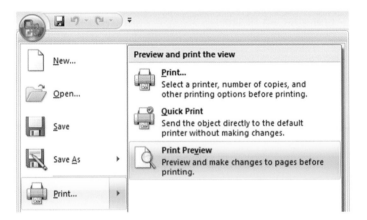

Adjusting Page Layout Settings

The Page Layout icon group contains powerful options to fine-tune your reports before you print them. If you would prefer to set your print options using a dialog, click the Page Setup icon.

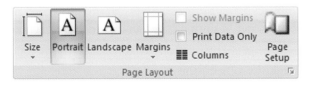

Printing Reports

As with most things in Access there is more than one way to
print a report.

Print Preview

 1   Switch to Print Preview

Print

Print

2   Click the Print icon

The Office Button

1   Click the Office Button

2   Click the "Print" menu item from the drop-down menu

Using the Print Dialog

Use this drop-down menu to
select the printer you want to use

Click here to set
printer-specific options

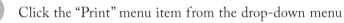

Print

Printer

Name: Xerox DocuPrint P12   ▼   Properties

Status: Ready

Type: Xerox DocuPrint P12

Where: LPT1:

Comment: ☐ Print to File

Print Range   Copies

○ All   Number of Copies: 3 ⬍

● Pages From: 1 To: 4

○ Selected Record(s)   ☐ Collate

Setup...   OK   Cancel

Click the Setup button
to specify margin sizes
and column settings

Click this radio button to
print a range of pages

Send Your Report via Email

Rather than print off your reports, you can now distribute them by email directly from Access. Not only that, but you can export the report in a variety of formats.

Hot tip

For more information on the Office Button refer back to page 12.

1 Select the report you want to email in the Navigation Pane

2 Click the Office Button

3 Select the "E-mail" option from the Office menu

4 Select the type of file you want to export the document as, using the Send Object As dialog

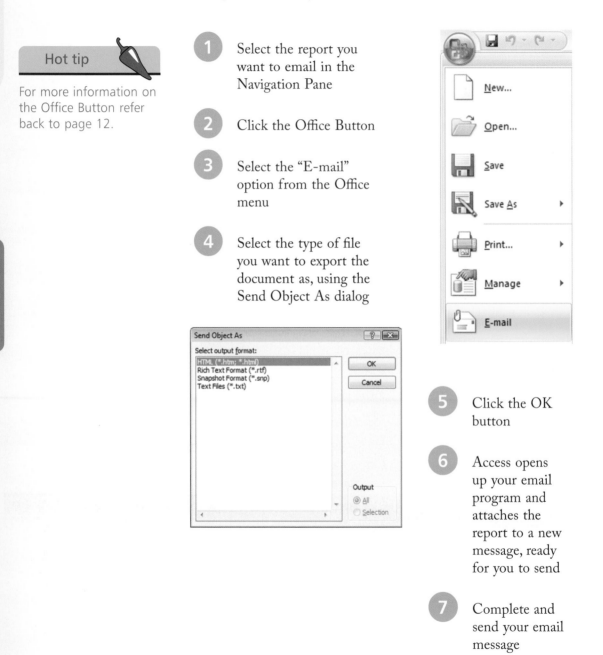

5 Click the OK button

6 Access opens up your email program and attaches the report to a new message, ready for you to send

7 Complete and send your email message

11 Sharing Access

The need for interoperability

has never been greater.

Luckily, Access makes it easy

to share data.

Password Protection

Sharing data between colleagues is generally considered a good idea, but there is always the chance of the confidential, highly sensitive records stored in your Access database falling into the wrong hands. To safeguard against the chance opportunist having a peek at your database, we can password-protect it.

Hot tip

Improve the security of your database by using obscure and impersonal passwords. Avoid using pet or family names. Good passwords are a mixture of random letters and numbers.

1 Make sure the database you want to password-protect is fully closed

2 Click the Office Button

3 Select Open from the drop-down menu

4 Use the File Dialog to locate the database you want to password-protect

5 Highlight the database but don't open it just yet

6 Click the down arrow to the right of the Open button

| Microsoft Office Access ▼ |
| Open ▼   Cancel |
| Open |
| Open Read-Only |
| Open Exclusive |
| Open Exclusive Read-Only |
| Show previous versions |

7 Select "Open Exclusive" from the drop-down menu

Clicking "Open Exclusive" forces Access to grant us the exclusive use of the database so that no other users can interrupt the task of password-protecting it.

8 Once the database has opened, click the Encrypt with Password icon located in the Database Tools icon group

9 Type the password you want to use in the top text field; then press Tab and type it again in the lower text field

10 Click the OK button

The next time the database is opened Access will ask for a password to be entered.

Removing Password Protection

To remove password protection click the Decrypt Database icon. To show you're not a malicious user disabling password protection, you'll need to enter the current password again.

Don't forget

The Decrypt Database icon can be found in the same place as the original Encrypt with Password icon. A database doesn't need to have been opened in exclusive mode to remove password protection.

Making an ACCDE Database

If your database is to be shared between colleagues or is to be used by more than one person it's a good idea to create an ACCDE database. An ACCDE database is exactly the same as your original one, except that users are not able to alter the design of forms or reports. Also, only Visual Basic for Applications code that was compiled will be included in the ACCDE database. Converting your original database to an ACCDE database is a great way of preventing users from accidentally damaging it.

1 Click the Make ACCDE icon

Make
ACCDE

2 Locate the directory in which you want to save the ACCDE file, using the File Dialog

3 Click the Save button

Remember to keep the original file somewhere safe. As your database evolves over time you'll want to make changes to it.

Backing-up Access Databases

There are many ways in which data can either be corrupted or lost. Databases could be completely erased by users, either accidentally or maliciously. Or an electrical spike could irreparably damage your hard drive. No computer is completely safe. You should always create regular backups of your data and store them in a safe place. Always store your backups on some form of removable storage, such as a CD-ROM or USB drive.

Do not back up your Access database to another location on your hard disk. This completely defeats the purpose of backing up.

 1   Click the Office Button

 2   Move your mouse over the Manage menu item

3   Click the "Back Up Database..." menu item

4   Use the File Dialog to locate the removable storage on which the backup will be stored

When saving your backup always make sure you add the date to the end of the filename, for example "Bobbin's Bank Backup 08/08/08". That way, you can easily find the most recent backup.

Splitting a Database

By splitting a database you can separate an Access database into a front-end file, containing all the forms and queries, and a back-end file, containing the tables.

 1 Open the database you want to split

 2 Click the Database Tools tab on the Ribbon

3 Click the Access Database icon

 4 Click the Split Database button

Database Splitter

This wizard moves tables from your current database to a new back-end database. In multi-user environments, this reduces network traffic, and allows continuous front-end development without affecting data or interrupting users.

If your database is protected with a password, the new back-end database will be created without a password and will be accessible to all users. You will need to add a password to the back-end database after it is split.

It could be a long process. Make a backup copy of your database before splitting it.

Would you like to split the database now?

[Split Database]   [Cancel]

 5 Use the file dialog to locate the directory in which to save the back-end file

6 Click the Split Database button

7 After a short while Access displays a dialog informing you that the database has been successfully split. Click the OK button to get rid of it

A split database can be used in exactly the same way as any other database. However, open up the Navigation Pane and you'll notice arrows pointing at the table names.

Updating the Back-End

1 Click the Database Tools tab on the Ribbon

2 Click the Linked Table Manager icon located in the Database Tools icon group

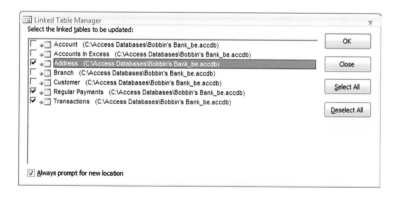

Hot tip

Check the "Always prompt for new location" box in the Linked Table Manager and Access will present you with the File Dialog every time you update the back-end.

3 Check the boxes for the tables you want to update

4 Click the OK button

Interacting with SharePoint

SharePoint Server is an application server that unifies an organization's web presence, intranet and business documentation. With just one server program it's possible to offer web content to the public, provide business-specific intranet content within an organization, and centralize business files and documentation such as Microsoft Word and Excel files.

Another useful feature of SharePoint Server is its snug integration with Access 2007. By using the import and export features of Access you can upload data to and download data from a SharePoint site.

A SharePoint site stores data as lists. The view of these lists differs according to user needs and permissions. When you upload a table or query to a SharePoint site it is converted to a list and when you download it, it is converted to a table.

Importing from or Linking to a SharePoint Site

Importing from or linking to data stored on a SharePoint site is similar to importing from other sources.

1 Click the SharePoint List icon in the Import icon group

2 Enter the address of the SharePoint site

3 Choose whether you want to import data from or link to a SharePoint list

4 Click Next

5 Choose the lists that you want to link to or import

6 Click OK

Index

E

F

R

S